IT'S ABOUT
DAMN
TIME

HOW TO
TURN BEING
UNDERESTIMATED
INTO YOUR
GREATEST
ADVANTAGE

IT'S ABOUT
DAMN
TIME

Arlan Hamilton

with Rachel L. Nelson

CURRENCY
NEW YORK

Published in the United States by Currency, an imprint of
Random House, a division of Penguin Random House LLC,
New York.

CURRENCY and its colophon are trademarks of
Penguin Random House LLC.

Library of Congress Cataloging-in-Publication Data
Names: Hamilton, Arlan, author.
Title: It's about damn time / Arlan Hamilton.
Description: First edition. | New York : Currency, [2020] |
Includes index.
Identifiers: LCCN 2020003066 (print) |
LCCN 2020003067 (ebook) | ISBN 9780593136416 (hardcover) |
ISBN 9780593136423 (ebook)
Subjects: LCSH: New business enterprises. | Entrepreneurship. |
Success in business. | Minority businesswomen.
Classification: LCC HD62.5 .H3555 2020 (print) |
LCC HD62.5 (ebook) | DDC 650.1—dc23
LC record available at https://lccn.loc.gov/2020003066
LC ebook record available at https://lccn.loc.gov/2020003067

Printed in the United States of America on acid-free paper

currencybooks.com

2 4 6 8 9 7 5 3 1

First Edition

Book design by Andrea Lau

To my mother, Mrs. Earline Butler Sims,
the real San Sebastian

CONTENTS

IT'S ABOUT
DAMN
TIME

From Food Stamps
to *Fast Company*

scending an escalator in a hotel I couldn't afford to stay in, I said to myself, "You are a venture capitalist. You are a venture capitalist." I had no home, no money, certainly no investment capital, yet I knew that was what I needed to say to myself. In order to become, I needed to *be*. I was sleeping on the floor of the San Francisco airport nearby; I came to this hotel to get a change of scenery and stay until they kicked me out. Then it would be back to the airport with my suitcase and backpack, back to the hard floor down from the Virgin Atlantic check-in desk, rolled-up jeans under my head for a pillow. I told myself, "You are a venture capitalist" as I checked my emails on the airport's free Wi-Fi, as I avoided the security people on their Segways, as I sent out yet another email asking for funding.

I was still spending days and nights at the airport when I wrote my blog post "Dear White Venture Capitalists: If You're Reading This, It's (Almost!) Too Late," which went viral in a matter of hours but still left me with no investors. It's been nearly five years since then, and now it's not just my staunch self-belief telling me I'm a venture capitalist; I literally *am* the founder and managing partner of Backstage Capital, a multimillion-dollar investment fund. I've invested in 130-plus start-ups with founders who are *underestimated* in the same way as I was, founders who identify as people of color, women, LGBTQ, or, if they're as lucky as I am, all three. In October 2018, I was the first Black female noncelebrity to grace the cover of *Fast Company* magazine.

In 2012, before I had even heard of the investment asset class called venture capital, before I was sharing hotel rooms with my mom, before I was homeless and sleeping in airports, in Airbnbs, and on friends' couches, I was a budding production coordinator in the live music industry, working for artists such as CeeLo Green, Jason Derulo, and Toni Braxton. I'd been at that level for just over a year when I started noticing that the successful people I looked up to, such as Ellen DeGeneres, Ashton Kutcher, and Troy Carter (Lady Gaga's manager at the time), were getting involved financially in the tech start-up scene. I wondered why those successful people with exciting lives and careers were spending so much time in a place called "Silicon Valley," making bets on tiny companies no one had ever heard of. I was intrigued by what the draw could be, so I started doing what I always do when I'm curious about something: I dived in, asking questions and researching. After that, I started reading books, any and all that I could get my hands on, about start-ups, venture capitalism, and investing. I had the bug.

From the outside, the world of start-ups, venture capital, angel investors, and limited partners (the institutions and individuals who invest in venture funds) looked like a meritocracy. That was what attracted me to it, and I'm sure it's what attracts a lot of people. The narrative around successful start-ups always seemed to follow a pattern of rags to riches: you hustle, grind, pull all-nighters, give your best every day, and finally . . . success arrives. As someone who has always been vision focused, who has always had big ideas and small re-sources, I became obsessed with this industry. I wanted to know everything about it, and so, I followed the money trail, and taught myself everything there was to know. Along the way, I learned some disappointing statistics. For one thing, 90 percent of venture capital was going to White men. That's a huge amount of money, given that tens of *billions* of dollars are deployed in venture investments each year. It means that 10 percent of venture capital is split (unequally) among all of the other types of people in society. As a Black gay woman who had been excited to enter into the exciting world of in-novation as an entrepreneur, I was more than disappointed to discover that something that had been sold to me as a meri-tocracy was actually a microcosm of the worst of society's biases.

I knew when I saw those statistics that the mythology around Silicon Valley was basically a lie, because ingenuity, hard work, hustle, grit, and innovation aren't traits that are prevalent only in the straight White male population. When talking about gender parity in VC funds and the gender pay gap, some high-level VCs talked constantly about hiring "the best person for the job" and about not wanting to "lower their standards" in order to accept women into higher-paid jobs. It's insane—not to mention incredibly prejudiced, misogynis-tic, and homophobic—to assume that the best of the best just happen to be 90 percent straight White males. Yet that was the assumption!

Historically, venture capitalists have looked to invest in founders who fit their idea of what a successful founder looks like, from their skin color and their clothing to their economic background and their educational status—and they don't even try to hide it. The legendary Y Combinator founder, Paul Graham, has admitted publicly that he can be "tricked" by a Mark Zuckerberg look-alike, and the successful and influential venture capitalist John Doerr went as far as to describe his ideal founders as "White male nerds." A lot of this is based on stereotypes that have been rife in popular culture for decades, especially when it comes to tech founders. Our biases ensure that we expect a tech founder to be a young White guy who attended—and possibly dropped out of—Stanford University or somewhere similar and started his company in his garage, because those are the stories we've been told by the media and those are the people we have seen be so insanely successful in the past decades: Mark Zuckerberg, Steve Jobs, Bill Gates, Jeff Bezos, and many others.

But if I thought that 10 percent number was bad, you can imagine how I felt when I learned that only one-fifth of 1 percent of all venture capital in the United States goes to Black women.

"HUSTLE" LOOKS COMPLETELY DIFFERENT DEPENDING ON YOUR CIRCUMSTANCES.

Logically, that made and makes no sense at all to me. In Silicon Valley, people talk endlessly about "hustle" and "hacking" your way to success. The thing is that "hustle" looks completely different depending on your circumstances. For most affluent White men, hustle might be pulling an all-nighter in front of a computer trying to get a project done; but for some of the people I know, hustle is sacrificing sleep to work on their side project after they've spent ten hours at their day job, come home and fed their kids and put them to bed, or checked on their elderly relatives, or before they start their night shift at their second job.

Look, I've taken the grapes off the stems in the grocery store so I could afford them, I've couch surfed, I've crowdsourced, I've bought a $1 doughnut so I could sit in an all-night doughnut shop when I've had nowhere else to go. And I've taught myself how to book countrywide music tours, built a magazine from scratch, and gotten myself backstage and onstage at some of the most influential business conferences in the world. I've hustled my whole life.

When I was deep into the journey to becoming a venture capitalist, my mom and I were roommates in Pearland, Texas, where I slept on a blow-up mattress. I barely left my room, spending all day and night reading books and blogs, watching YouTube videos made by successful venture capitalists, and sending emails. When I couldn't afford to buy a book, I went to Barnes & Noble and sat there reading until closing time. I sent hundreds of cold emails to investors, asking to intern for them, asking to work for them, asking if they would mentor me, asking if they would hear me out. Save for the extremely rare positive response, I was met with a barrage of nos or was blatantly ignored.

It didn't deter me; there's never been a time in my life when one person's no has made me give up entirely. During that same period, I started coming up with ideas for funds. First I wanted to start a million-dollar fund for LGBTQ founders. I went out to all these angel investors and asked for backing, but nobody would touch it. Nobody even thought it was anywhere close to being necessary or viable. I worked on things like that for months, but they didn't come together. That was while I was still working my other job and trying to make ends meet.

I looked for new avenues, and in April 2015, after more than three years of researching and reaching out to Silicon Valley from a distance, something substantial finally came out of it. I was accepted into a pilot venture capital education program put on by the well-known start-up accelerator and venture fund 500 Startups and hosted at Stanford University. Partially through the help of a crowdfunding campaign— kick-started by a $500 contribution from Chris Sacca, a VC billionaire who didn't know me well at the time but wanted to help, and bulked up by amazing friends, family, and strangers who threw in $5 to $100 each—I bought a one-way ticket to San Francisco. I was going to Silicon Valley, and no one was going to stop me.

That was a huge turning point for me. I already knew I was passionate about helping to change the disparities in the amount of capital going to underrepresented founders through VC, and I knew I wanted to be a part of an industry that took risks and encouraged innovation and entrepreneurship. But it wasn't until I attended that class that I realized just how unique my value proposition was. I was one of only two Black people in the class, and notably, the class— spearheaded by 500 Startups partner Bedy Yang—was about 50 percent women. We were encouraged to write blog posts about Silicon Valley and start-ups from our unique points of view, and when I looked around, it became obvious what I needed to write about.

WHAT IF THE NEXT MARK ZUCKERBERG IS A LITTLE BLACK GIRL FROM THE SOUTH?

Just as with stocks, companies, or horses, betting on the people everyone else is betting on is not often the savviest way to do things. In fact, it can be quite lucrative to bet on the underdog. That was the thesis behind my blog post "Dear White Venture Capitalists: If You're Reading This, It's (Almost!) Too Late." I wanted to turn the idea of pattern matching for "White male nerds" on its head and instead use pattern matching to my advantage; I was looking for people who reminded me of myself. At the time, I couldn't get the thought out of my head: "What if the next Mark Zuckerberg is a little Black girl from the South?"

The fact that so many people were being overlooked made no sense to me. I was talking to a lot of underrepresented founders, and I saw how much they were struggling, as well as how much they had to offer. I also saw what they were achieving with the tiny amount of resources they had. Venture capitalists blamed the lack of diversity in their investments on pipeline issues, meaning that they weren't meeting investors who didn't look like them. So I started reaching out to investors and founders who were *not* straight White men. Over time, I began helping to connect those people with one another, which in turn connected founders with funding.

It seemed really natural to give more funding to people

who could do more with it and to find great deals for people who had money but didn't have differentiated or interesting portfolios. It made sense to me that just as underrepresented founders often didn't have access to the social circles where networking happened, investors didn't have access to all of the founders I was meeting. They weren't seeing all the untapped potential that I was seeing, and it made sense to me to act as a bridge.

I didn't go to college, and everything I knew about venture capital I learned myself, at home, with a whiteboard, handmade index cards, and that blow-up mattress. So I guess I could understand why maybe I wasn't taken seriously initially. But then I spoke to other Black women who were graduates of Ivy league universities, who had MBAs, who had years of experience in tech, and who were the breadwinners not only for their immediate family but for their extended family, and *even they* were being ignored and overlooked by venture capitalists. Those who did get meetings and introductions told me about the numerous times they had been grilled about their educational history or their work experience, how they had to prove they'd attended the school on their résumé, how they had been asked if they could "handle" raising children and running a business (when was the last time a VC had asked that of a guy? I wondered). At least half of the meeting would be taken up by convincing the investor that they were qualified just to be in the room.

I thought about what it would look like if I invested in people like me; women, people who identified as LGBTQ, or people of color. Those groups of people were all underrepresented in Silicon Valley and the start-up world, and I could identify with each one. It was something I had a personal experience with; they were people I already had links to, could relate to, and understood deeply. Not only would it be a personally satisfying way to approach venture capital, it would give me an edge. As the saying goes, "Go with what you know."

I hadn't planned to join the industry as a venture capitalist; after all, I had absolutely no capital, and I'd been in debt most of my adult life. But the more I learned about the start-up world, the more I liked it and wanted to be a part of it and the more the venture capitalist asset class—this relatively small sliver of private equity that was built to fuel massive innovation at the earliest stages—seemed like the perfectly aligned tool to help me achieve my mission.

I'd always had ideas, I'd always felt like an entrepreneur, but my ideas either hadn't led anywhere or hadn't brought me success. When I discovered Silicon Valley and heard about all the ups and downs that founders went through, their failures and successes, it reminded me of myself. But I soon realized that if there were going to be more founders who looked like me, there would have to be more people who looked like me writing checks. A lot of founders go through what is called a "friends and family" round of raising money when they first begin a start-up. Most underrepresented founders I know don't have that kind of luxury where their dad can throw $25,000 at their summer project. So it hit me: What if I could create a fund that would act as their friends and family round?

Back in the summer of 2014, after I had done hundreds of hours of research and talked to dozens of people, I made a decision. It happened while I was pacing the parking lot of a Comfort Inn where my mom and I were living in Pearland, Texas, thinking "What am I going to do next? Am I going to start a company? Or do I start a fund, which sounds so crazy to me right now, but at the same time, I've been working on it, and I know the players, and I know the rules, so maybe I should give it a try?" I'd asked a few people who know me well what they thought, but it hadn't really helped. So I paced and paced, and finally I said to myself, "You know, I could start a company, and I could probably hack my way to raising for it because now I know all these inside secrets from talking to VCs and to founders. Or I could start a fund that touches hundreds of founders and hundreds of companies; what would that look like?"

I'm asked all the time: "How do I know whether or not I should keep going or give up on this company or this project or this mission?" My answer is this: If you close your eyes and visualize the world five, ten, twenty years from now and feel okay with the thing you're working on not existing, then it's not urgent. But if you can't imagine the world without it and want it to exist whether you get to enjoy the benefits of it or not, then not only is it important to you, it is your calling.

So on that summer day, I suddenly stopped pacing and asked myself, "Imagine it's five years from now [2019] and this investment fund does *not* exist. Can I live with that?" I kept my eyes closed and let my imagination run wild. The world was moving quickly; I was out of poverty and happy. My family was doing well. As a species, we'd made great strides in tech in just a few short years. But in the image I conjured up in my mind's eye, in a world where this fund didn't exist, something was missing and definitely awry. Black, Brown, women, and LGBTQ founders were still not getting their fair share and were not being taken seriously. They still were not a large part of the decision making that would go on to determine how thousands of products and services would be built and distributed. They were still not as wealthy as White men were. They still had to justify their existence in spaces that should be for everyone. Furthermore, they still had to ask for permission to excel.

My eyes shot open. That was not the world I wanted to live in five years later. The answer was clear: I'm going all in, and I'm not going to stop until I have a venture fund that invests in underrepresented founders.

Once I knew what my mission was, I knew what Backstage Capital would be. I sent out more emails, met with more investors, heard more nos. When I talked to other VCs about my idea for the fund, I generally received one of two responses. The first was a smile, a sort of patronizing pat-on-the-head attitude, and something along the lines of "That's nice, what a great thing you're doing for underprivileged people." The second was skepticism that I would have the quantity and quality of deal flow—that I'd find enough companies and be allowed into enough deals—to justify raising a fund. It seemed crazy to me; had those people ever left their homes or walked down the street? Did they live on the same planet as I did? Women make up more than half the population, and I dare anyone to argue that White men have the market cornered on good ideas, innovation, vision, or execution. Women alone would create enough deal flow for a fund to invest in for the rest of my life! People of color are a minority in the United States but a growing one; the 2017 census put the percentage of White (with no Hispanic or Latinx background) citizens at 60.7 percent, which means that people of color make up nearly 40 percent of the population. Meanwhile, one in ten people identifies as LGBTQ, and that number is growing. Need I go on? How can there not be a wealth of talent, entrepreneurship, business savvy, and innovation to choose from among these groups?

Another excuse I became familiar with was "I don't understand the market." This is rooted in the bizarre belief that underrepresented founders serve only underrepresented customers, and the White men I met with viewed those markets as somehow "niche." But in reality, underestimated founders are just as likely to make a product or capture a market that serves a large swath of the population.

Those responses are indicative of how Silicon Valley as a whole seemed to think about underrepresented founders, whether they said it out loud or not; as though we were charity cases or not up to a certain standard. They were basically asking "Do Black people, women, or LGBTQ people have the ability to build venture-backable companies?" I wanted to tell them that I intended to run a for-profit business that could make both me and others very rich. I wasn't looking to give handouts; I was looking for return on investments. Yet there are still a lot of people who hear about anything that involves "diversity" or "underrepresented groups" and think it's about giving a helping hand; they see us as a subpar option that you choose to feel you've done "something good." The assumption that underrepresented means underqualified, unaccomplished, inexperienced, or unskilled not only is false, it also shows how far we have to go to change the idea of what a successful founder is.

I came to realize that women founders, LGBTQ founders, and founders of color aren't just underrepresented, they are *underestimated*—a phrase coined and gifted to me by one of the founders I've invested in (and wordsmith!) K. G. Harris, during my fund Backstage Capital's two-year anniversary event in San Francisco. That's true not only in the start-up world; these groups have been systematically underestimated in one way or another in just about every field. So in 2015, I made a promise to myself that I would invest in one hundred companies by 2020, not as a vanity metric but as a proof of concept. I was seeing those companies, I knew they existed, and with a little time, capital, and effort, they would have their moment. I'd soon come to see that there were other people with checkbooks who believed that, too. Marlon Nichols, Troy Carter, and Suzy Ryoo at Cross Culture Ventures; John Henry at Harlem Capital Partners; Kesha Cash and Stefanie Thomas at Impact America; Aaron Holiday at 645 Ventures; Monique Woodard at 500 Startups; Charles Hudson at Precursor; Austin Clements at Ten One Ten; and Freada Kapor Klein and Mitchell Kapor at Kapor Capital are just some of the investors I'd soon meet and work closely with.

Getting Started

My very first investor was a woman named Susan Kimberlin. Susan was an angel investor, which meant she would be taking a risk with her own money, and I think as a woman she really understood the pain point. My only hurdle was convincing her that with no background, no Silicon Valley connections, and no capital on the horizon, I was going to be able to invest in the hundred companies I was claiming I was going to invest in by 2020.

Imagine you're her, meeting me in 2015. I'm homeless and have no money (you don't know about the homeless part, but you do know about the no money part). I am thirty-four, so around the same age as you, and I should probably have it together. I don't dress the part, I don't look the part, I don't have the background. I don't have the references. I didn't go to college. I don't even have my own bank account. All these things, and I'm coming to you and saying "Hey, I want to start a venture capital fund and I want to invest in a hundred companies that are led by women, people of color, and LGBTQ+ people." With your money.

But she stuck with me, believing in me, daring to imagine what I could do. She waited until I had a business account set up and a top-tier lawyer and had proved to her that I was serious and could learn quickly. Then she sent me an email that changed my life with two simple words: "I'm in."

> I WANT TO SHARE THIS JOURNEY
> NOT BECAUSE I THINK I'M EXCEPTIONAL,
> BUT BECAUSE, LIKE MANY PEOPLE,
> I HAVE BEEN EXCEPTIONALLY UNDERESTIMATED.
> AND IF YOU'VE PICKED UP THIS BOOK,
> I'M GUESSING THAT SO HAVE YOU.

After dancing in a grocery store parking lot, I was officially in business. My mom had already suggested I name the company Backstage Capital as a callback to my days in the music industry. She said, "You help musicians get ready for the spotlight behind the scenes; maybe you'll do the same with founders." Obviously, my mom is a genius. I loved the concept! Over the next few years, I began to hire a team, most of whom came to me and wanted to work for Backstage. I called them the Crew, and our founders were our Headliners. Since then, so much has happened in both the micro and macro. I invested in more companies, raised more money, secured some high-profile investors, and faced my debilitating stage fright to go on to speak at many conferences. Oh, and the people who laughed or scoffed at me in 2015 and said I wouldn't invest in one hundred companies by 2020 were partially right; Backstage Capital invested in its one hundredth company two years early, in May 2018. And here's the thing: I'm just getting started.

SELF-BELIEF ALONE WILL NOT ACHIEVE YOUR GOALS, BUT ACHIEVING YOUR GOALS WITHOUT SELF-BELIEF WILL BE ALMOST IMPOSSIBLE.

I want to share this journey not because I think I'm exceptional, but because, like many people, I have been exceptionally underestimated. And if you've picked up this book, I'm guessing that so have you. I want my story to empower you, and I want my story to inspire you. I want to give practical advice, tips, hacks, and positive mantras that you can apply to your life now, rather than just ask you to visualize your wish and hope it comes true. Self-belief alone will not achieve your goals, but achieving your goals without self-belief will be almost impossible.

This book is for anyone who has felt boxed in by other people's expectations, who has been told to be smaller, to take up less space, to stop asking "Why?" It's for anyone who wants more than society has allotted him, her, or them. It's for all those who have ever been told they "don't have what it takes" to do the thing they're passionate about, whether that thing is graduating from college, starting a company, rising to a position of leadership, publishing a book, having their face on the cover of a magazine—you get the picture.

But it's also for the allies, the men with privilege who use it to help those without. It's for anyone who wants to understand how diversity could be our greatest superpower. It's for those who want to learn what life is like for someone with a different background from theirs, with experiences that aren't a part of their norms. A rising tide lifts all boats, and I want the tide to keep on rising and lifting up people who have spent their life being underestimated by those with power, connections, and money. This book is about change. It's not just time for change; it's about *damn* time.

This book is divided into eight parts: becoming money, relationships, resilience, authenticity, creativity, confidence, self-care, and the big picture. Each part will tell you a little about my journey and experiences, my past, and my hopes for the future and will give you advice you can put to use in your own life and on your own journey. These lessons are not just applicable to investors, founders, venture capitalists, or those interested in Silicon Valley; they are foundational life lessons that I hope will help you access the best of yourself. We all have it in us to do more than we are currently doing, we all have things that are holding us back, whether it's society's view of us or our view of ourselves. If this book helps you change the way you think about yourself and others, if it helps you dream bigger than you used to, I will have reached my goal.

I will be transparent about my successes and failures, my highs and lows. And by talking about all the doors that I had to push my way into, I hope to open the door even wider for you. I hope to help you understand that all the people in the room are humans just like you are: that they are your equals and not one of them is inherently "better" or more deserving than you. I'm here to show you that you don't have to be a genius or the absolute number one at everything to achieve success. If you take away only one thing from this book, I hope it's the knowledge that no matter what you do for a living or where you are in your career, you deserve to walk through the door of any room you want to be in.

PART I

BECOMING MONEY

1

Let's Get (In)formation

Most successful people will tell you that money attracts money. This means that something about what you're doing or the process you've put into place continues to help your money and assets work for you even when you're not working. These people will tell you that that's when you know you've attained success: if you're able to make money while you sleep. When money is working for you, you are not working for money.

So what do you do if you have no money? I'm now in my late thirties, and for thirty-five years I had no money. I grew up with no money, and in fact I have had massive debt my entire adult life. How did I begin to attract money? I believe that if you have no assets, *you* have to become the asset. You must become not just valuable but undeniably *invaluable*. And the way to do that is through having more knowledge about your corner of the world than anyone else.

Whenever I'm introduced at an event or people meet me and hear about my journey, I'm asked how I did it, what my secret is. How did I go from sleeping at the airport to getting the first yes? The answer to this question is a combination of things: grit, tenacity, conviction, hope, determination, and earnestness about my mission. But the engine that powered it all was *information*. I acquired information and then wielded it as needed.

We are lucky to live in a time when information is widely available, whether on your phone or laptop, through membership at your local library, by using the internet at a friend's house, or by sitting in a hotel lobby and using its free Wi-Fi (I've done all of those things). If you're lucky enough to have access to some of these—and most of us are—you have just about every piece of information available at your fingertips. This has become so normal that it's hard to believe that just twenty years ago, it was not the case; instead of Google, we had things called encyclopedias that today we look back on as artifacts!

Some people assume that knowledge is available only to those of us who read voraciously or who naturally love to learn. This is *not* the case. People acquire knowledge in different ways, and all types of learners can discover and use the knowledge they gain to their advantage. I was never someone who could sit down and curl up with a good book; then I discovered audiobooks, and I started learning much more much faster, because the method worked for me.

During my time as a music production coordinator in 2012, I began to be insatiably curious about Silicon Valley. As it always does, my curiosity turned into research, and that research turned into a passion for the start-up world. Back then I was working for various artists and was on and off tour, so I met a lot of people from different backgrounds of whom I could ask questions and from whom I got all kinds of different and interesting answers. I also had a lot of downtime when I was on the road that I used for reading and learning.

Sometimes people ask me what gave me the confidence to think that I could be a venture capitalist when everything and everyone was telling me I couldn't. Honestly, the answer is that I fought insecurity with information. Remember, I spent the years 2012 to 2015 reading everything I could get my hands on. Every single day, I read blog posts, books, magazine articles, and newspaper clippings; I listened to every podcast I could. I did that day in and day out for years before I ever got one check. (Another key is I never stopped! I still do that to this day.)

At the same time, I knew that there are certain types of knowledge you can't get from books and podcasts; you need to talk to people who know things, and to do that, you need to start making connections. I knew I wanted to get in touch with Sam Altman, who was then the president of Y Combinator, a successful accelerator program for start-ups (remember I mentioned his predecessor Paul Graham in the intro), but I didn't have any access to him. So I did the uncouth thing of reaching out to his brother, Jack, and asking if he could connect us. I found Jack's info on LinkedIn after doing ten or so minutes of online research on Sam. Unsurprisingly, Jack said no, so I asked if I could send him my pitch deck instead, and he said "Sure." The next day, he messaged me and told me he was going to put me in contact with Sam, because he knew his brother would want to see what I was planning. He got Sam to give me a call, and after our long conversation, Sam sent me a text that read, "The world needs what you're doing. I want to help."

He put me in touch with a lawyer who turned out to be one of the biggest fund formation attorneys there is, and for the next year, the lawyer worked with me for free and taught me so much. That made me feel confident enough to start approaching investors, angels, fund managers, and private family offices, all the while continuing to ask questions, gather information, and educate myself on this new world and how it works.

To this day, when facing a big decision, the first thing I do is read about what other people in my situation have done. So if I'm facing something challenging with my company, I'll imagine that maybe somebody else has gone through the same kind of thing. If we're talking about a specific topic, I'll look it up, I'll research it. That always bears fruit, because then I can see the different ways that history has already been written. How did it go when handled this way? How did it go when handled that way? Taking that information, how can I apply it to my circumstances? Sometimes I reach out to people I know have gone through similar things, and I interview them.

If you're a founder or an aspiring founder or you're one of the first twenty or fifty employees at a company, and you're facing a dilemma or are wondering *Should I take that next role? Should I go to the other company? Should I quit my job and start something?*, it's helpful to talk to other people who have been in your shoes. Talk to people who are in your shoes now. You're not asking them to tell you what to do, you're gathering data. All of this is about gathering data, assessing it, analyzing it.

I can't tell you the number of times I have been in a conversation with someone who has already been a venture capitalist for years, and that person is asking *me* questions as if I'm the savant, because they did not learn the way that I did. I had to learn from scratch. I went from having never heard of the industry, to having only the vaguest of ideas about what it was, to having to know as much as possible about it so that I could play with the real players who were doing real deals. If I was going to spend other people's money, I would have to be ready.

And I was. Because every time I read a book, every time I listened to a podcast, every time I went through another twenty handwritten index cards, every time I learned more about the key players, I was building my intellectual capital, my war chest of information. Over time, I have become known for having this knowledge. Now people come to me and give me thousands of dollars to give them bits of information, thus saving them months of research time and tens of thousands of dollars, to give them insight, to give them inspiration. They're paying me, and I have no formal education; no degree, no business school, not even an evening college class. I learned everything I know from reading, listening, watching, and being intent on learning. I learned from relentlessly consuming information that is available to everyone. I dedicated time and effort to the thing that fascinated me, and I found a way into this business by using my knowledge as capital.

In other words, I became the money. I became the attraction. My mind, my information, my brain trust became the assets. Since becoming a little better known, I've been asked by aspiring founders and investors if I will act as their mentor. It's a total full-circle moment because it wasn't so long ago that I was the one emailing as many people as possible asking for mentorship. I would love to mentor everyone who reaches out to me. But since there's only one of me, the way I'm doing that is through projects such as this book. And as you've already read in my story, I got way more nos than yeses, so those years where I had to figure things out on my own were an amazing training ground for when I was introduced to the powerful attorney who elevated my education and status. I wouldn't have been prepared for what he had to teach me if I had been introduced to him earlier in the process and had not learned so much on my own. This to me means that if you're asking people to be your mentor today and it's not going well, repurpose that into a positive thing. Become your own mentor for a while. You can always learn more.

Don't get me wrong: I'm not just here to tell you, "Hey, you have the power to go out and google everything and make a student of yourself and learn what you need to know." My goal is to provide you with the tools and resources you need to do so. That's why everything we've done with Backstage Capital has had an element of both learning and teaching. Check out the section of our website dedicated to learning resources, The Green Room, where we discuss all things start-up and investment; the *Bootstrapped TV* YouTube channel, where we show you what it looks like behind the scenes; and now *Your First Million,* an indie podcast where I interview successful people about how they reached their first million, whether dollars, subscribers, downloads, or customers. I'm doing all of this for you, but I'm also doing it for me, because in teaching this stuff, I continue to learn on a daily basis as well. In fact, colleges and universities have now reached out to have me speak and/or teach! I have spoken at Yale, Columbia, Berkeley, Cornell, and Oxford. I have been asked to become a visiting professor at Duke/UNC. There was a Harvard Business School case study written about Backstage and me in 2019. It all stemmed from independent research and learning using the same tools that most of you reading this have at your fingertips today.

Remember, when Beyoncé says, "Okay, ladies, now let's get in formation," she's also saying "Let's get information." Indeed.

2

Skip the Rehearsal

got into touring when I was twenty-one. I was working at a bank doing ten-key-by-touch check encoding, which is exactly as boring as it sounds. The one good thing about the job was that I could listen to music all day. I came across a Norwegian pop-punk band called goldenboy, and I liked their music (based on the one song I had heard at that point), so I got in touch with them online and said, "I want to see you play live." They replied, saying, "Well . . . we're in Norway." And I said, "Okay. Well, if I book some shows here, will you come here and play?" And they were like "Sure. Okay." I'd wanted to be a part of the live music business since I was thirteen years old, and my boredom at work mixed with my enthusiasm for that band was the perfect cocktail to push me into action.

Back then we weren't using Google to figure stuff out; instead, I kept a physical folder for each city on the floor of my family's apartment and used an actual phone book (like, as in the yellow pages) to look up venues. Every Wednesday, I would call a few up, ask for whoever the production manager was, usually Griff or Buzz or whoever, and say, "Hey, I'm trying to book this Norwegian pop-punk band." I didn't know a lot, but every time I had a conversation, I'd learn another word, another phrase from the jargon, another piece of the puzzle. And so within a few weeks, I was saying things like, "Look, Snake, if we don't get twenty percent of the door, we walk." Faked it 'til I made it. The first few people I spoke to were like, "What are you talking about?," but eventually I got the hang of it. It was not easy, but through trial and error, I booked goldenboy a multicity summer tour across the country.

I was their tour manager, culture translator, babysitter, and confidante. Just five fair-skinned Norwegian dudes, and one Black American woman, crossing the United States in an old van. The guys loved the weather here, so they were constantly taking their shirts off. And they loved how cheap the beer was, so every time we got to a new town, they would storm into the grocery store topless and buy crates. Then we would arrive in the next city, open the van door, and all these empty beer cans would fall out and five topless dudes would emerge. It was cute and everything, but in certain cities I had to give them a reality check before we got there. For example, when we were going to places such as Little Rock (at the time), I would say to them, "We have to have some ground rules for this city, because if anything happens, I'm the one they will arrest. So I need you to be cool." That's the reality when you're a Black tour manager in the South.

Don't get me wrong, I was having an absolute ball. We didn't have any money; they had drained their bank account to get to the United States and managed to scrape together just enough cash to buy the used van I'd lined up for them, so we had to be hackers a lot of the time. We would play a show, get the $50 or $100 from the door—meaning our measly share of ticket sales—sell some CDs and T-shirts, and use that money to buy gas to take us to the next city. Then we'd book one room in a motel, and Nils, the bass player, and I would go to the counter and we'd say, "Hi, yes, we are a newlywed couple, we'd like to get a room . . ." Nils would be drunk and sweaty, but he also had an amazing command of the language and an impressive ability to pull himself together, especially once I made him put a shirt on. While we were distracting the desk clerk, the others would lug all the stuff from the van into the motel room, and every night we slept five or six people to one room. We didn't have much money (or privacy), but honestly, we were having the time of our lives. They were drunk every night, acting like the fun-loving rascals they were, but they were always respectful. You wouldn't guess it to look at them with their colorful spiked hair and occasional tattoos and piercings, but they were teachers back in Norway and truly lovely guys. Personality-wise, they were more pop than punk, and I loved it.

After the second cross-country tour, we mostly went our separate ways, save for a Christmas or New Year's Eve together here and there, but Nils, B.T., Torkel, Gaute, and Jostein are still friends to this day, eighteen years later. Those kinds of experiences will bond you for life. We were all young and learning together; I was becoming a tour manager through sheer willpower, they were on their first-ever tour across the United States. We were all faking it until we made it and teaching one another to dream bigger. In summer 2019, golden-boy released their first new album in years, called *Adult Dis-*

oriented Rock, and dedicated the lead single, "Old and Boring," to me. Their liner notes describe the song as such: "Old and Boring" is an ode to ourselves, our former manager and now super-hero-venture-capitalist Arlan Hamilton, and above all, our lifelong friends and fans who have been following us from the start. It is about the effort you make and the fun you have, playing in the same band for 20 years. It is the story of a seemingly random group of young men turning into old, grumpy men, going everywhere together and ending up nowhere. Or somewhere. We celebrate the rehearsals, the friendship, the backstages, the clubs and the lovely people we have met along the way!"

Sending love across the waters.
Hard to stay apart, need one more, is this the end for us?
Kinda hoped that this would be eternal.
Last time I saw you, was in the Wall Street Journal.
Never ending happy endings.
Going home alone, this is just another song . . .
Look at me, I'm telling myself stories.
Oh, I guess that we're just old and boring now.

Fast forward 41, still remember how much fun.
Back when it all begun, it surely felt like such a run.
Big applause in Little Rock, Stillwater and Stoli shock
And California sun. . . .
Still missing Ocean Beach, the next big tour seems outta
    reach.
I'm down here on my knees, I try to practice what I preach
Still I'm playing my guitar, the kids have been put safely
    into sleep.

Imagine what it could have been . . .

I can still remember every night
You stood up and saved me from that fight
Dancing on the rooftop of our van in Chicago
After our worst show, all these memories
Hard to let go . . .

3

You Need Only One "Yes" Out of a Hundred

n 2010, I was looking for a way to get back into the music industry and level up my skills in terms of tour size and job sustainability. I was living in Los Angeles after having bounced around among many different cities: Columbus, Dallas, Jackson, Chicago. I needed some kind of cash flow, so I'd started picking up gigs as a production assistant on various reality TV shows. It was okay and paid around $150 a day, which was incredibly impactful at the time, but there was no long-term financial security. Each gig only lasted one or two weeks, and it took a long time to find each one. Plus, there were no benefits included, which of course meant no medical insurance. I'd applied for a lot of different long-term jobs, but I hadn't had any luck and was getting to the point where I couldn't afford my rent, so I took on two roommates, a young couple, maybe nineteen or twenty years old, two men from Minneapolis. They were adorable, cute as a button, but they also got into awful fights; they'd argue and become violent, my stuff would get broken, and then they would make up, smoke weed all day, play a lot of Rihanna, and dance around.

Anytime Rihanna was playing, it was a good indication that they were "making up." All would be calm, and then, sure enough, the yelling would begin again, one of them would stumble into the living room with a bloody nose, and eventually they would make up . . . you get the picture. I'm no prude, but I was a grown woman and I had to get them out of there, for all of our sakes. Problem was, without their rent checks I couldn't afford my place.

I needed a plan of action. I knew I loved working with touring artists, so I decided to reach out to tour managers and production managers. Being on the road would solve two problems: I'd be getting paid, *and* I'd be traveling, staying in hotels or motels paid for by the artists. That would allow me to ditch my lease, put my few possessions into storage, and finally save up some money. When you're starting from less than zero, this is an attractive option. I wanted to be smart and intentional in my plans, so I decided I would send out exactly one hundred emails to prospective tour managers and production managers at different levels of production, from House of Blues tours to arena tours. I'd only ever toured with artists in cars and vans. But I knew I could handle the bigger tours because I'd done just about everything except perform or handle the tech on the previous tours I'd run. Entry-level work on a larger tour would give me a chance to work my way up to tour managing an arena artist, which at that point was my ultimate goal.

The first step in my plan was figuring out whom to email. I looked up artists I respected and found out who their tour managers were, googled extensively, and went through who knows how many email addresses of people I'd met over the past decade; I even looked for archived copies of physical tour books, which were pre-internet records of all the people who had worked on different tours. The hardest part was finding email addresses for the names I had; sometimes I had to get creative with my searches or make some assumptions to find them. I got a free trial of an expensive trade magazine, used it every day for the fourteen days I had it for free, and then canceled it before I had to pay.

Once I had compiled a list of one hundred names, I began writing emails. I didn't want to send the exact same email to every recipient; I figured some of those people were bound to know one another, and I didn't want to risk their comparing emails and thinking that I didn't care. I wanted to get across how passionate I was about the business, about finding an opportunity. I needed them to know that I knew their names, not just who they worked for and what was on their résumés, and that I respected them. It's really important when you're reaching out to a large group of people with the same agenda that you honor their individuality and reinforce it with your own. Taking the time to understand who the person on the other end is as a human being has to be at the core of all your interactions, whether with business contacts or in your personal life.

I began writing emails. I couldn't realistically write a customized letter to everyone, asking about their family and telling them about mine, but I made sure I personalized at least one of the first sentences, showing each recipient I knew who I was emailing and had picked them with intent. I would mention something I'd read or noticed about them or a song or concert I liked, based on the artists they had worked with.

I tried to be as detailed as possible when constructing that first part of the email.

I would then describe my previous experience and the opportunity I was looking for. At that point, I'd worked on maybe a hundred shows (!!) with indie artists but never on a tour of the scale these professionals were running. I knew it was important to be truthful about that fact. It wasn't just the fact that back channels exist in every industry and community, ensuring that any dishonesty could come back to bite me. I have always valued my integrity, and so lying was not an option. Instead, I made sure to highlight my real accomplishments, even if considered small at that point. I explained that in my previous role, I had booked the shows *and* managed the tour—that I had scheduled the route, organized the logistics of the tours, and managed the artists' day-to-day needs—because I wanted them to understand how dedicated I was, how seriously I took my work, and the professional lengths that I would go to learn the craft.

All of that was true, too. I loved touring, not for the exposure to famous people or the glamour or the money. I love music, traveling, being exposed to different cultures and learning from them. Not only that, live music and travel catered to the kind of people I loved, people who were passionate and creative. I needed to be around those people—my people—again. I wanted to be true to myself and completely authentic. I hoped that one of those one hundred managers would be looking for someone just like me.

I chose to send one hundred emails because of the math. I knew that the odds of the majority of people even reading the email, let alone responding to me, were low. I knew that those who did read it might relate to me or find what I had to say interesting. Of those who did, most would not be looking to take on any new hires or would be hiring only from within their own network. Timing is everything, and for some people, the timing just wasn't going to be right.

Of the one hundred tour managers and production managers I emailed in 2010, twenty responded. Three asked for or agreed to an in-person meeting, and *one of those three meetings* turned into an actual opportunity. Luckily, that one was enough.

Geoff Perren is a UK-born world traveler with an amazing track record working with major artists: David Bowie, Marilyn Manson, Prince, and Lauryn Hill, among many others. He's been touring for more than forty years. He does not mince his words, he does not suffer fools gladly, and he is quite a character. The best way to describe him is as if Rod Stewart, Archie Bunker, and the Crocodile Hunter morphed into one person. Meeting him was scary, because he says exactly what he thinks and has no time for nonsense. But what most people don't know about Geoff is that he is also one of the sweetest people you could ever meet. He is an absolute teddy bear once you get to know him, especially if he respects and trusts you. We met at a Beverly Hills Starbucks; he was catching a red-eye to England in a few hours. We talked; he seemed kind of grumpy, and I couldn't tell if he liked me or not. I knew that he could probably help me break into the industry, and I was nervous because of how high the stakes were for me, but I was still very confident. I needed him to understand that I could hold my own if I did get the job.

In the middle of our meeting, he had to take an important phone call; while on the phone, he needed a pen and didn't have one, and I noticed that and immediately found one for him. He didn't have to skip a beat with the person he was talking to, because I saw his needs and dealt with them without his telling me to. He noticed that, and it made a difference; it showed that I cared, was aware, and could anticipate other people's needs. Being ready for anything, going above and beyond, and not waiting to be asked to do something if you see it needs to be done are key assets regardless of whether you want to go into the touring world, get your first gig stocking shelves at a grocery store, or close a million-dollar deal.

Geoff became my boss and mentor, but it didn't happen overnight. At the end of our meeting, he told me, "You know, we're not looking for someone immediately, but I did want to talk to you and get to know you." I said, "Okay!," and that was that. I didn't know if I would ever hear from him again, because I still couldn't tell if he liked me. Besides, I could have been just one of many people he had interviewed or spoken to that week.

I heard from Geoff the next day via text about something mundane, and then, a few weeks later, I moved back to Houston, Texas, to live with my mom. She was leaving a relationship at the time and needed a fresh start, and it was a lot easier for both of us to afford a place together. So we got a two-bedroom in Houston. It was exciting for us because it had been a long time since we had had our "own" place, even if we didn't have much furniture. We had a couch in the living room, my mom had a bed and a TV, and I had an inflatable mattress on the floor of my bedroom. We weren't sure how we were going to pay the rent on a monthly basis because neither of us had a steady job (though my mom was technically retired and so received a pension), and paying the deposit and first month's rent had taken all of our savings. But for the time being, at least, the place was ours.

One night in late December 2010, we headed out to a gas

station down the street to get some snacks. I'd been kind of depressed by my situation, and the holiday season had compounded the feeling. I was thirty years old, and I couldn't understand how I had ended up in this situation. I remember thinking I didn't have much to look forward to. As I waited for my mom to grab some snacks, I got a text message from Geoff, asking, "You busy the first week in January?" I replied, "Nope!," and he said, "I need you to meet us in New Orleans"—"us" being the CeeLo Green band and production team. "I need you to meet us in New Orleans in January and I need you to do a show."

I was over the moon. When he said, "I need you to do a show," he meant I had to organize everyone's travel, help with the logistics and execution of getting everyone to and from venues, and essentially attend to the needs of everyone in the touring party. It was going to be high pressure, I was going to have a lot thrown at me at once with very little setup time, the stakes would be high, I would be stressed to my limits—and I was stoked!

I had a few days to sort all that out and learn everything there was to know, and I was determined to be ready. I said to myself, "You know what, this could end up bad. I could do a bad job and mess this up. But if I do well, this could be the beginning of something incredible: a career that I have wanted my entire life." I knew I had to figure it out. A few days later, I watched CeeLo sing on TV at the Times Square ball drop on New Year's Eve, knowing that the next week, I would be one of the people backstage and I'd be watching my new boss perform live.

The two or three days I spent in New Orleans were like boot camp. There were two shows with several musicians from England, a lighting director, a front-of-house engineer, a tour manager, CeeLo's career manager, people from the record label, people from the management company, a guest DJ (DJ Ruckus), a guest singer (Eric Benet), and all sorts of friends and family. I had to hit the ground running, and I did. Along the way, Geoff peppered me with quick lessons as though he were Mr. Miyagi and I was Arlan-san. Except that his "Wax on, wax off" was more like "Who left the fucking printer at the fucking hotel?" and "Where the hell is the goddamned promoter?" Aw, Geoff. I really do miss it.

I went on to work for CeeLo for another couple of years, and some of my fondest memories come from that time. Unfortunately, in 2012, accusations of sexual assault were made against CeeLo. Although he has denied the accusations and was acquitted, I left the team to pursue other opportunities.

Meanwhile, Geoff Perren remains a good friend and mentor. More recently, even though we hadn't seen each other in quite a while, he texted me and said something dry such as "Saw your magazine cover, kid. Well done. So who's going to play me in the made-for-TV movie?"

MILLIONS OF DOLLARS LATER, NOTHING CAN COMPARE TO THAT FIRST YES.

It can be so frustrating and demoralizing at the beginning of a career, a start-up, or a new venture, when you just want to be given the opportunity to prove yourself and all you seem to get are nos. When I was looking for investors in Backstage Capital, I heard so many nos before I got a single yes. But once it came, that first yes was incredible. It meant more than money; it meant that someone other than me (and my mom and my friends) believed in me. It meant that despite all those people saying no, all those people laughing in my face, all those people telling me my idea was not sustainable or not worthy of investment or that the founders I cared about were only charity cases, someone shared my vision. I will never forget that first investment, not because of the amount but because of its impact. It was the one that made my dream of creating greater access to capital a reality. Millions of dollars later, nothing can compare to that first yes.

It doesn't matter how many people say no or ignore you, as long as you get one yes. Lady Gaga has been sort of poked fun at recently for saying this often in interviews for her film *A Star Is Born*. But it's so true, and I'm living proof. You need only one to get to the next round, the next level in the video game of life. And when you do, you'll find that that yes can lead to another yes. Not only that, sometimes the nos still lead to a yes further down the line. I can't tell you how many times I've been given a no, only to find that a better, brighter, bigger yes was around the corner.

After working with CeeLo, I went on to work with many other artists, including Toni Braxton, Jason Derulo, and Janine (formerly known as Janine and the Mixtape). I traveled to Aspen, the United Kingdom, Abu Dhabi, Paris, and Vancouver and all over the United States. I set the foundation for a successful career for myself as an arena-level production coordinator and indie tour manager, and it all began with those one hundred well-planned, thought-out emails.

4

There Is No Such Thing as Self-Made

Though I am the first to stand up and tell the world I am a hard worker, have grit, think "outside the box," and am self-reliant, I would also be the first to let you know I am not "self-made." No one is. I have not met, seen, or heard about one single solitary founder, executive, leader, or successful person in the history of the world who has done everything on their own. The idea of the self-made person is romantic and perhaps helps some people to strive and push themselves to do more, but overall I find it to be a damaging myth. It encourages the idea of the lone genius, the outlier, and can create an impossible standard to try to live up to. The idealization of individualism does not appeal to me. Yes, I am my own boss, and I thrive when I am the one making the decisions that affect me, but I am nothing without the community that surrounds me.

I HAVE NOT MET, SEEN,
OR HEARD ABOUT ONE
SINGLE SOLITARY FOUNDER,
EXECUTIVE, LEADER, OR
SUCCESSFUL PERSON
IN THE HISTORY OF THE WORLD
WHO HAS DONE EVERYTHING
ON THEIR OWN.

I am made up of every person who believed in me, who took a moment to respond to an email, who listened to me talk about my ideas, who made sure I ate something after a long day. I am made up of my mother, who raised me to understand there was nothing I couldn't do. I am made up of my brother, my wife, my friends, and certainly every member of Backstage Capital's Crew. It would have been impossible for me to do what I have done alone. Whether in start-ups and venture capital, the music and entertainment business, or anywhere else, success is a team sport. It can't be achieved alone, and that's the reason an infrastructure exists. A start-up may begin with one person's idea, but it can expand past the idea phase only with the help of other people.

Most of the people who claim to be self-made had a lot of "ins" already: they knew someone who set them up with an internship or got them an interview, or they attended a private school, where they met people who would later help them out. I think to say you are self-made is the most egocentric thing there is; it's a belief that you are living in a bubble, that you think the things you do and say are more important than those of the people around you. If someone claims to be "self-made," they are telling you that they're the kind of person who does not acknowledge their partners and co-workers. And who wants to work with someone like that?

BE HUMBLE, ACKNOWLEDGE THE HELP YOU ARE RECEIVING, AND THANK THE PEOPLE AROUND YOU.

Be humble, acknowledge the help you are receiving, and thank the people around you. The fact that you can't get where you are going alone is a great thing; it means you don't have to struggle on quietly or give up, you can ask for help! And when you are successful, pay it forward: hold out a hand and help other people up. I believe that we, especially underestimated people, are stronger together. We have a duty to help one another. Instead of claiming to be "self-made success stories," wouldn't it be great if we could hold ourselves up as "community-made success stories"? That's the kind of community I want to be part of.

Here are a few tips on how to lift up fellow underestimated people:

- Recognize the underestimated and make space for those who are underestimated for different reasons than you are. Diversify your team, your friendship group, your community.

- Listen to them. Underestimated people have untapped potential; they have great ideas that are rarely heard because they are never given respect. When you're speaking to fellow underestimated colleagues or friends, give them your full attention.

- Amplify the voices of those without a microphone. If you have the power of a voice that can be heard, use that voice to name-drop underestimated people whom you admire. Give credit where it is due, and highlight people who are not yet household names in their field of expertise.

5

Write Your Own Headlines

Back in 2015, I wrote a draft email that said "Backstage Capital Invests in 100 Companies!" Of course, at that point Backstage Capital was not even a fund, it had no investors, and it had certainly not invested in any companies. But that was the future I wanted for my company; that was the headline I wanted to see written about us. I set the date for the headline as 2020, and I knew that I'd achieve it.

Writing my own headlines is something I've been doing for several years in one form or another. Think of it as a pocket-sized vision board. I wrote the headline in 2015, and in the years that followed, every time I looked into my draft folder, I saw it staring back at me. It was a reminder of what I was aiming for and something that helped to keep me on track with my goals.

In May 2018, we reached that goal, way ahead of schedule. Not only that, the headline I wrote in 2015, which I predicted would be a statement of fact by 2020, actually showed up on the *Fast Company* website as a real headline! I'm not claiming that simply writing down a goal will automatically bring it to fruition. But it does keep you pretty damn focused and motivated to achieve it.

WRITING YOUR OWN HEADLINES IS A GREAT WAY OF GETTING CLOSER TO *MAKING* YOUR OWN HEADLINES.

Of course, your headline doesn't always turn out to be accurate. Sometimes, for some reason or other, you don't reach your goal. Sometimes you reach it in a way that you never imagined you would; the end result is different from, maybe even better than, your prediction or your hopes. But that's really part of the magic, because you're setting yourself up to walk toward the future that you want to see exist. It helps you have clarity about what you want in life. What do you want? What do you want to accomplish? What would be exciting to read about yourself in two or five or ten years? This way of planning for the future and setting goals has helped me create a target that is achievable and clearly defined, rather than a collection of vague wishes. Writing your own headlines is a great way of getting closer to *making* your own headlines.

PART II

RELATIONSHIPS

6

Optimize for People

Networks—the connections between people that turn into webs of friends and acquaintances—are everywhere. Networks are, without a doubt, incredibly important and always have been. They've been around forever: private members' clubs, fraternities and sororities, golf clubs. They're church groups and book clubs, and they're groups of bar regulars, social groups, and the PTA. Sometimes networks provide you with information about snow days, and sometimes they give you a job. They vary a lot, and they are not equal in the kinds of benefits they provide.

WHEN YOU DON'T HAVE
MANY RESOURCES,
NETWORKS AND RELATIONSHIPS
CAN BE VALUABLE CURRENCY.

When you don't have many resources, networks and relationships can be valuable currency. Relationships are one-on-one; networks are how you tie relationships together, and understanding how to navigate both is an important skill. Some people have a natural ability to relate to others one-on-one and genuinely create a connection with them; other people are good at connecting people to other people who can help them. If you can do both, the world will be your oyster.

When you tour with musicians, you can't help but learn about relationships and networks. When I was working on my first indie tour with goldenboy, we'd go to a city for the first time and five people would show up for the show. The next time we came, there would be fifteen; those five had all told a couple of friends about the band. But you have to be prepared to build slowly; no one becomes a rock star overnight.

By working with countless indie singer-songwriters, pop musicians, rappers, and rock bands, I've studied the way artists build that connection and network of fans for two decades: taking a picture with every person after the show, reaching out to fans to come and see you when you're playing the support slot for another artist who has a slightly larger following. It's a groundswell. In 2003, I discovered that the child and teenage actress Jenny Lewis was in a band called Rilo Kiley, which was playing at a small venue in Columbus, Ohio, where I was living with my good friend Sarah at the time. Jenny had starred in some of my favorite childhood movies, such as *Troop Beverly Hills* and *The Wizard,* and later she had gone on to star in one of Angelina Jolie's first movies, *Foxfire.* Now, as a grown-ass woman, she was going to be playing rock music nearby? Be still, my little lesbian heart.

It wasn't a big gig, but each musician in the band gave everything on that tiny stage. The place was so small that

Jenny had whiskey with a lot of us after the show—and even remembered me and said hi by name a few months later, when I went to see her in Dallas (thus helping me score major coolness points with a date I'd brought to the concert). In 2019, I saw her play in LA at a five-thousand-capacity, standing-room-only, sold-out venue, at least thirty times the number of people at the show in Columbus. And it's all related. Jenny and her band reached out and touched the lives of every soul who came to see them at those early shows. They showed love to the people who showed them love first. And over time, that organic connection—plus the consistent delivery of high-quality music—has paid off. Jenny can fill a monster venue with people who love to come out and see her doing what she loves, and she has been able to stay true to herself in the process.

I've seen this happen with talented musicians for all of my adult life and have taken those lessons with me into Backstage Capital by trying to make genuine connections with each and every person who has supported us since the beginning. It's not just the people with the checkbooks (such as our limited partners and other venture capitalists) and not just the founders whom we're counting on to return that investment and then some. Backstage Capital is part of a movement; people are interested in what we're doing, they're following our progress and become part of our network because we represent something larger and more important than just ourselves. Founders know that we won't be able to invest capital in every person we meet, but we want to be real with them, we want to be in the moment and connect to them.

7

Be Insatiably Curious About People

Every time you meet a new person, you have an opportunity to learn something. I have met thousands of people in my life. I've always found them fascinating, I've always wanted to know more about people who were different from me. Your relationships with others—whether your significant other, your friends, your neighbors, your work colleagues, your boss, or total strangers—have a major impact on your life. Relationships matter more than money, more than status, more than material things. In any given situation, what makes an experience good or bad is the people involved and your relationship to them. It's impossible to overstate the value of keeping relationships healthy and treating people well.

Connecting with people has always been important to me, but it hasn't always been easy. Even as far back as kindergarten, I was not a fan of small talk, and I remember struggling to relate to a lot of what the other kids were talking about. I didn't play with them much; I was strong but clumsy and not athletic, so I wasn't drawn to any of the outdoor games. Instead of playing, I spent my time sitting on the sidelines thinking about how the other kids were feeling. Our playground in elementary school had big concrete cylinders you could sit inside for shade or crawl through for fun. Each of them had a baseball-sized hole you could peek through and watch what was happening on the playground. I would sit in those cylinders, look out at the other kids, and observe how they behaved, how they interacted with one another, and how they reacted to different situations. I'd think about their home life and imagine what their house looked like, what their family was like, if they were happy. I'd imagine what they would be like when they grew up, what kind of adults they would be. I was endlessly curious about what other people were thinking; I was fascinated by thoughts, knowing that we all had them and that no one else could see them or take them away. I spent a lot of time alone thinking about thinking. I was kind of a weird kid!

By second grade, I began to hold what I now think of as "Arlan's Office Hours" out of those cement cylinders. I'd beckon classmates over to come and sit with me at playtime, and I'd ask them, "How are you feeling? What's going on at home? What do you want to be when you grow up? How did you feel last week when Robby pulled your hair?" I loved to have those kinds of conversations that connected me to people and taught me about how their minds worked and how their lives were different from mine.

In the third grade, I wore six watches, three on each arm, set to six different time zones. It blew my eight-year-old mind that there were people in another part of the world who were seeing the moon while I was seeing the sun. I was—and in many ways still am—in awe of it all. Not only was I amazed by the fact that there were people in other parts of the world who were sleeping while I was awake, it also helped me to feel connected to those people who were so far away. This was long before the internet was available in everyone's pocket, before talking to people thousands of miles away was the norm, and wearing those watches made me feel as though I were on a special adventure, a citizen of the world, rather than just a little kid in Dallas. I don't know why at that age I felt I needed to be connected to people in other countries, but it's something that has stayed with me my whole life. It has always been important to me to look beyond my own circumstances, surroundings, and culture in order to understand the world and myself.

> WHEN THE MAJORITY
> OF THE WORLD LOOKS
> AT YOU AS "OTHER,"
> IT BECOMES IMPERATIVE
> TO CONNECT WITH
> PEOPLE WHO HAVE
> THE ABILITY TO
> SEE YOU AS YOU.

As I got older, my need to connect grew. For anyone who has ever felt like an outsider, the drive to "find your people" becomes unstoppable. As a gay Black woman raised as a Jehovah's Witness (*formerly*), I felt like an outsider all of the time. When the majority of the world looks at you as "other," it becomes imperative to connect with people who have the ability to see you as you—people who are the same as you in some way, whose first impressions of you don't stem from assumptions regarding race, gender, or sexuality. I've always been interested in not only finding my community but also helping other people find theirs. Many of the projects I've been involved in have been based on community. I published an indie print magazine and a blog, each for years of my adult life and both of which were aimed at queer women in some way. The best things that came out of those adventures were the things I learned about people through the communities I'd created.

Way back when we were all still using MySpace, I used my platform there to suggest that maybe women who were interested in women could wear some kind of coded item to enable others to identify them. That would help them meet each other and would avoid the fear of "Oh, God, am I about to hit on someone who is interested only in men?" I suggested we all wear a purple string around our wrists, and for a few years, many people around the world actually did! I loved knowing I'd made that impact, that I'd started something that went beyond people reading my words. Over time, my blog, *Your Daily Lesbian Moment!*, became the impetus for dozens of friendships and romantic relationships. Women wrote to me constantly to tell me they'd met their best friend on the site or their current girlfriend or wife. Some even moved from different countries to be together after meeting in the comments section of my personal blog.

Back in 2004, I was working on my magazine, *Interlude.* I poured my heart and soul into that magazine, and I loved it. The first issue was ready to be printed, full of beautiful photographs, interviews, and other interesting content. The only problem was, it turned out that printing a coffee table–type magazine is very expensive; I needed $10,000 to print the magazine, and I had run out of money. When you don't have money and you don't have access to people who *do* have money, you have to think outside the box. Some ideas will work and some won't, but no matter what, you have to use your initiative and ingenuity. If you want to be an innovator, these two things are essential. So is keeping things legal!

At the time, I was temporarily staying with my mom and her husband in Houston, Texas. I wasn't feeling great about myself. Despite how much I loved blogging and writing, I was pretty unhappy, because I was at an age where I felt I should have been much further along in life. I wanted to have accomplished more and be more independent. Times were lean; I didn't know anyone who had $10,000 lying around, and I couldn't get a business loan. If *Interlude* was to have a future, I would have to think of another way around it.

I've always been something of a hacker. I don't mean this in the identity theft/election meddling sense. I just mean I've always looked for a way of doing things that was different from the norm, because I never felt accepted as part of the norm. That time my hack came in the form of a quest: I would challenge myself to meet ten thousand people in person and take a photograph with every single person I met; then I would post the photographs—along with everyone's names and what number they were on my quest—on a website for people to check out. I designed and printed a T-shirt that said WORLD CITIZEN that I would sell on the site, and I would also have a donation link on there, in case anyone wanted to contribute to my quest. My thought process was: if I make a $10 profit on each shirt, and just one-tenth of the visitors purchase a shirt . . . voilà.

I remember working out how I would put the plan into action. I thought, "Okay, if I can meet three hundred people a day, this is a two-month operation at most." I was going to begin in Houston, but I thought that maybe once the project gained some traction, I might be invited to other places to meet people. I didn't know where any of it was going to go, but I knew I had to try.

On the first day of my quest, I headed to an alternative gay neighborhood in Houston. I charged my inexpensive digital camera overnight and made sure the memory card was empty. Then I borrowed my mom's car and parked outside a bar. My plan was to go in and introduce myself to a big group of people (so that I wouldn't have to begin by explaining myself over and over again), take a photo with each of them, note their names and numbers, and move on. I figured if I did that all day, I'd manage three hundred, no problem. I knew people would probably think I was weird, but that didn't really bother me. Let's not forget, I was the eight-year-old who went to school wearing six watches. Plus, it made sense to me that if people were in a bar at 2:00 P.M. on a weekday, we might get along anyway. Having some liquid courage at my disposal wouldn't hurt, either.

I entered the bar, ordered a drink, and headed out to the back patio, where the lighting would be better for taking photos. I approached a group and introduced myself: "Hey, I'm Arlan, and I am on a quest to meet ten thousand people this year. I'm taking a photo with everyone that I meet, and I'm putting them on a website, which you can check out." There was a slight pause, and I braced for the worst. Then one of them said, "Oh, awesome. That sounds great. Let's do it!" and they all looked at one another and then got in line to have their photo taken with me. Other people started noticing and asking what was going on, so word spread around the bar quickly, and those who were interested came over to meet me.

Things were going great. "I'll be done with this in no time," I thought. What I hadn't anticipated was that I might end up in a really long conversation with every five or six people I met! What happened was, I would introduce myself to them, and because I was doing this weird thing, people wanted to know more about me, which made me want to know more about them. I didn't anticipate that people would actually care and want to engage with me, and I also underestimated my natural curiosity about—and need to connect with—other humans living on this rotating rock.

That first day, I met a woman who was probably around twenty years old, having coffee across the street from the bar. I went over to introduce myself, told her what I was doing, and because it was a quieter situation in the coffee shop, we got to talking. She was in college, and she told me that her dream in life was to work as a researcher and therapist with orangutans using art therapy, specifically painting therapy. She told me she was studying sociology and behavioral sciences, and I said, "Wow, that's really amazing." I thought that was such a niche dream. We took the photo, and I moved on, thinking I'd met the most interesting person of the day.

I continued my journey, working my way down the street talking to people and taking photographs, and I met all types of people: Black, White, Latin, Asian, Indian, men, women, straight, gay, all sorts of people with all sorts of interesting stories and backgrounds, all with differing reactions to what I was doing. Later that afternoon, I walked into a restaurant, still in the same area, no more than half a mile from where I'd started. I talked to a group of people, and I said my now well-rehearsed spiel: "I'm Arlan. I'm on a quest to meet ten thousand people. I'd love to take a picture with you. You can go to the website in a couple of days, and your picture will be up," etc. I met a woman who was in her forties, we started talking, and I asked her what she did for a living. I will never forget that moment. She said, "I work with orangutans on painting projects for therapy."

Once again, my mind was good and blown. I had just met a college student who had wanted to do that her whole life and had been just half a mile down the road a couple of hours earlier. I told the woman what had happened, assuming that maybe they knew each other, but they didn't. She couldn't believe it either; the two of us were dumbstruck. I said, "You know, what's wonderful is that she's going to go to this website, hopefully in a couple of days, and you're going to go to the website, so maybe you'll be connected. I'm going to write a little something about this, and I hope you meet each other." To this day, I don't know what happened to either of them, but I've always hoped that they connected and helped each other out in some way.

THERE ARE THREADS THAT CONNECT US ALL, AND ONLY BY BEING INSATIABLY CURIOUS ABOUT OTHERS CAN WE DISCOVER THEM.

After several hours of meeting people, I went home. When I looked through the photos, I couldn't believe it. I had been aiming for three hundred people, and I'd actually met . . . thirty. I had hugely underestimated not only how much time it would take but also how emotional I would feel about the experience. I had learned so much from talking to those people; we had discussed their lives, their dreams, their families. More than anything, I had learned that when you let your curiosity about people prevail, you see that people who may look and seem completely different from one another actually have more in common than meets the eye. There are threads that connect us all, and only by being insatiably curious about others can we discover them.

That exercise, on the first day of my ten-thousand-person quest, was one of the most life-changing and mind-expanding days of my entire life. I was so grateful for it, and the challenge of making $10,000 to publish the magazine, while still a priority, was no longer as important. I still needed to raise the money, but it didn't have to be done that way, because this felt like a higher calling, something that was worth the time that it was going to take. That was fifteen years ago, and even then I'd noticed that we rarely look up long enough to make eye contact with strangers on the street. We're even more isolated now that cell phones are such a huge part of our lives. We are *connected,* constantly, in different ways. But truly *connecting* in this way—that felt special.

I went on to work on my quest over several months, with a lot of delays and breaks in between when life got in the way. I ended up meeting approximately five hundred people in Boston, New York, Dallas, Los Angeles, and Ohio; I made a YouTube video about it, which you can still see if you look up "Arlan's 10,000 Quest."

I never got to ten thousand, but I still want to; I'm sure I've met ten thousand people in my life, but not in the same way. I hope that one day I get to continue this quest; we learn so much about the world and about ourselves when we open ourselves up to other people. I may have stopped counting, but the spirit of the project lives on in the connections I make with people every day and the connections that others make through me.

8

Let Someone Shorter Stand in Front of You

At thirteen years of age, I went to my first concert. It changed my life. Janet Jackson was performing, and I was a big Janet fan; I knew all the lyrics, I watched every music video, and I was desperate to see her live. I loved her music, of course, but there was something about the way she carried herself, the way she spoke in interviews that captivated me. She was a wealthy Black woman being herself no matter what other people said about her or to her, and I found that incredibly inspiring. She was also just so damn *cool* and talented. Here I'd just like to note that contrary to what my friends and family assume today, I never actually had a crush on her. She was aspirational.

When I heard that she would be performing at the amphitheater in Dallas, where we lived at the time, I begged my mom to let me go to the concert, but she told me we couldn't afford it. So I tried to save the money myself. Little did I know that my mom had secretly bought me a ticket—just one for me, because she couldn't afford two. It was in the lawn seats, pretty far back from the stage, but I didn't care. I was so excited and grateful. Then, a few days later, I serendipitously won a ticket to that very concert by calling in to a radio show and answering a question about Janet's music. I knew every song, so that part wasn't difficult. But I nearly lost my mind when they said I had called in at the perfect time and was the 104th caller. I couldn't believe my luck; now I had an actual seat instead of lawn general admission, even though I would still be far from the stage.

My mom drove me to the show, put some hoop earrings on me to make me look older so no one would wonder why a thirteen-year-old was attending a concert alone, and gave me a talk about not letting anyone know my real age and not taking candy from strangers. She sat in the parking lot for the whole evening while I had the time of my life, and I can never thank her enough for that.

I was really excited about the show, so I got to the venue early. I found my seat and started talking to a guy and a girl in the seats next to mine. They were teenagers, probably only two or so years older than I was, but it felt as though they were so far ahead of me. We were all giddy with excitement and talking at a mile a minute, saying things like "Did you see Janet on this show?" and "Did you see she did her hair like that?" and "Well, Janet says . . ."

Pretty soon, a guy in his thirties approached us and said, "You guys are here early. You must be big fans." We looked at him as though he had just made the most obvious observation imaginable, and said, "Well, yeah, of course, it's *Janet*." He smiled and said, "Well, how would you like to watch the show from the front row?" Immediately my mom's voice echoed in my head; I informed him that I knew all about people like him, I knew he was trying to steal my ticket or run some kind of scam, and I was *not* going anywhere with him. He said, "How about you hold on to your ticket, walk down to the front with me, and if I'm lying, you still have your ticket and you can just come back to your seat?" I thought that sounded reasonable, plus we had a little time to kill, so, adjusting my earrings, I followed him, along with my two new friends, down to the front row. It was a pretty long walk, and I remember being certain that someone who worked at the venue was going to stop us as we got closer and closer to the stage. But everyone just smiled as we walked past them. Then, when we reached the front row, the usher took the dude's tickets, gave him a knowing look and smile, and said to us, "Have fun!" as he pointed us to our new seats. *What sorcery is this?* I wondered. I was in the front row of my first concert ever, seeing my musical idol perform live.

> THAT FREEDOM TO DREAM
> AS BIG AS YOU DARE,
> THAT'S SOMETHING
> MONEY CANNOT BUY.

We watched the whole show from the front row, and it was honestly life changing. Whenever I took a break from screaming my butt off for Janet (though clearly I didn't take enough of them, given that I had no voice the next day), I looked back at the audience to take in the moment, the huge amphitheater full of people of all races, genders, ages, orientations, all of them singing the same lyrics at the same time. We all had at least one thing in common: we all loved this powerful, immensely talented Black woman. She transcended age, sexual orientation, and creed. The feeling was indescribable: the intensity of experiencing a live show for the first time and having the best seats in the house. I didn't quite understand what the feeling was, but I knew I had to find it again and never let go. I understand now that it was a natural high. That night, I learned I could dream bigger than I was dreaming, and that realization, that freedom to dream as big as you dare, that's something money cannot buy.

PRIVILEGE IS A HAND-ME-DOWN HEIRLOOM . . . ; ENTITLEMENT IS SOMETHING YOU PROCURE AND CHOOSE TO WEAR.

We found out later that the man who had given us the front-row tickets was Janet's husband at the time, René Elizondo, Jr., and Janet liked to have him do that sort of thing for fans. Janet was all about sharing her privilege, but at scale. Here's the thing about privilege: everyone has it, to some degree. I think when some people hear the word *privilege,* they get defensive, but I'm here to tell you that having privilege, or being privileged, is not the problem. Entitlement is the problem. I think of it this way: privilege is a hand-me-down heirloom, rooted in the circumstances you're born into; entitlement is something you procure and choose to wear. There is nothing wrong with being privileged, as long as you use your privilege to help others who lack it. It's as if you're at a concert and someone shorter than you is standing behind you and can't see the stage; you would probably move aside to let them stand in front of you, right? It's only a slight inconvenience, you didn't get any shorter, and you *both* get to enjoy the show.

Using your privilege to help others doesn't take anything away from you, especially when you have it in abundance.

USING YOUR PRIVILEGE TO HELP OTHERS DOESN'T TAKE ANYTHING AWAY FROM YOU.

The best thing about having a new perch now is that I'm now in a position to pay this gift forward, and that's exactly what I'm trying to do in Silicon Valley and beyond. My aim is to siphon the privilege of those I come into contact with and the privilege I gain and redistribute it to people who need it. I want to share the access I have to help founders find someone to take a chance on them. I call it Augmented Privilege™. We can all do this in our own way; we all have some kind of privilege, and it's our responsibility to use what we have to help those who don't.

In 2017, I went to see Janet in Anaheim. I'm lucky enough to be able to afford the good seats now. I bought two extra tickets, and prior to the show, I walked around the venue, looking for someone to give them to. It felt amazing to approach a woman and her mother and give them the same speech I'd heard at thirteen: "Come down to the front, and if I'm lying, you still have your ticket." It felt even *more* amazing experiencing the show with those two women nearby, seeing their excitement and joy and knowing they wouldn't forget that night for a long time.

Having the opportunity to see that show at all, never mind watching it from the front row—well, I'm not exaggerating when I say it changed the trajectory of my life. After that first concert, I became even more obsessive about music, and I realized I wanted to work in the live music industry. I was chasing the energy I had felt that night.

By age fifteen, I was already putting the internet to good use and tracking down Janet's tour manager. I knew who he was because I'd seen him on MTV, and eventually I found his email address and we began to talk on AOL Instant Messenger. Now, it doesn't sound great to say that this man was chatting with a fifteen-year-old online, but I promise you it was innocent. I said to him, "I want to do what you do," and once I convinced him that I was going to be a tour manager, he agreed to put me on the guest list for a show happening at the same venue where I'd seen Janet. He sat me backstage, and for an hour, I watched everything happen. The headlining band couldn't find their drummer (they thought he might have ended up in the wrong city), and someone else had lost his parrot. Yep, you read it right, his parrot. It was another world. Eventually they found the drummer (but not the parrot), and once they were ready to go on, I got to walk with them to the stage and watch the show from the side. The feeling of walking with an artist to the stage before a show is still a thrill, no matter how many times I've now done it. It's one of the best parts of the night for me.

At the end of the show, the tour manager turned to me and asked, "Are you sure you still want to do this, kid?" and I said, "Absolutely, more than I ever have before. This is it. This is magic." I was certain. Those two nights in that Dallas amphitheater, two years apart, put me onto a path.

I don't doubt that it was the experience of seeing myself represented on that stage—combined with the experience of being backstage—that gave me the confidence to edge my way into the music industry. I wanted to be on the inside, and I knew I could be. It was all right there in front of me.

I hope that if you take away one message from this book, it's this: You can do it. You deserve to be backstage, on stage, and in the front row. And once you make it there, don't forget to let someone shorter stand in front of you.

9

Agree to Disagree

speak on a lot of panels, and I take part in events. Unfortunately, I am often the only Black person or the only Black woman onstage. It's almost as though there's a one-in-one-out policy, and not only that, it's usually the same handful of successful Black women who are asked to speak. We see one another at these conferences and compare notes on who is speaking at which diversity panel that particular day. It can feel as though we are interchangeable with one another, the token member of the panel. Case in point: I've been confused with, referred to as, and introduced as other Black women entrepreneurs in the past.

What this means is that there is rarely a chance for people in our profession to see us disagree. If someone mistakes you for another Black entrepreneur, that says something about their knowledge of you and your beliefs. The best way to make your beliefs known and to stand out and be remembered (for reasons other than your gender or skin color) onstage is to take a strong stance on something that not everyone up there agrees with.

I was once asked to judge a pitch competition at SXSW, and when I walked into the venue, I found I was the only Black woman judge. Having been asked to be there, I used my clout to insist that another Black woman be added to the judging panel or I would not do it. When the organizers agreed, I went and grabbed Melissa Bradley, a prominent investor, and brought her up to the stage. The organizers found her a seat, and her unique perspectives and opinions added a whole new dimension to the information that was being offered. Melissa had expertise in areas I had no background in and was able to give great feedback to the competitors that made the competition so much better. Instead of focusing on our "diversity," we *diversified,* and as a result, we improved.

Here's another example of how diversity of perspectives and opinions can matter so much more than diversity in the traditional sense. When the editor of *Zora,* a Medium publication that features reflections and perspectives on the lived experiences of women of color, invited me to write a weekly dedicated column for them, I asked if instead I could carve out my own corner of the publication in which I would introduce many different women of color in the tech industry to the readers by inviting them to write their own pieces. That meant that instead of readers hearing just *my* voice, they would hear from a wide range of women of color who in many ways had more experience in tech, while people who might not otherwise have had the chance to be featured would now get a platform.

WE'RE NOT ALL CARBON
COPIES OF ONE ANOTHER,
WE'RE NOT A BOX TO TICK,
AND WE'RE INTERESTED IN
AND PERFECTLY CAPABLE
OF SPEAKING ON TOPICS
OTHER THAN DIVERSITY.

I'd like to see more panels on which there are multiple people of color so we can be on different sides of an argument about cryptocurrency or fund legislation, so that people know that we're not all carbon copies of one another, we're not a box to tick, and we're interested in and perfectly capable of speaking on topics other than diversity.

PART III

RESILIENCE

10

The Road Trip That Lasted Forever

My mom taught me all I needed to know about resilience. She grew up in Jackson, Mississippi, in the 1950s and '60s. She is a survivor of a great many things, some of which came from simply living as a Black woman in the South in that time and some of which are more personal. She was my first hero, she's my hero to this day, and she's also my best friend. I have an overwhelming amount of respect for her.

I grew up always feeling loved, cared about, and cared for. It wasn't until I was in my late thirties— the age my mom was when I was five or six—that I really understood that she hadn't *had to* keep my brother and me, stay with us, or treat us the way she had, with such love and care. Growing up, as kids tend to do, I took all that as a given, but I now understand that she had other options, ones that someone else in her position could easily have chosen.

Her life changed when she had my brother and me, and though she raised us alone, she took care of us the best she could. For a period of time when I was a teenager, she had to work more than one job. I remember how she would come home from her day job in telecommunications, make us dinner, and then head out to her second job, working overnight at 7-Eleven. She hacked her way through parenthood in the true sense of the word, and I definitely learned a deep work ethic from her. It wasn't always easy. We definitely butted heads because we are so much alike, and we sometimes argue because we're both so stubborn. But I haven't met a mother and daughter who care for each other and have never argued!

I grew up in Dallas. I went to Lake Highlands school from kindergarten through senior year of high school, but we moved apartments at least half a dozen times during that period. I was lucky that we moved within the same area so I had the stability of attending the same school no matter what, and that definitely helped when our housing situation was the opposite of stable. We moved for a number of reasons: there were some break-ins, and once there was a physical assault (something we don't talk about). I remember one time, in my late teens, we moved because we were in a *better* financial situation and we were actually upgrading. The place we moved into had a garage and a bonus room, and I remember thinking that we had made it! It was really cool, and although it didn't last long, I was proud of my mother for creating that experience for us.

My mom and I used to call ourselves Thelma and Louise because we would often find ourselves in a rental car driving from city to city or place to place within one city, staying on friends' couches or in hotels. We were on a never-ending road trip because we didn't have any other choice; we didn't have any permanent living arrangements, we were both struggling for stable employment, and we had to make do with whatever we could. We turned it into a bit of an adventure to help ourselves cope, because it wasn't an easy path and it took our pride away, you know? It wasn't the easiest thing to ask family members if you could stay with them for a while. I spent more time in Jackson and on my aunt Clothilde's couch than I can count. My mom was in her forties, fifties, and sixties during that time, and I was in my teens, twenties, and thirties. I think both of us felt that we should be past that part of our lives.

My brother was fighting his own battles during those times. He left school early, had children, and built a beautiful family, but he has gone through a lot of ups and downs with his own money issues, making a few poor choices, as teenagers do, and outside of that, having an experience with police brutality that was completely out of his hands and not his fault. But he is a hacker if ever there was one; he took adversity and turned it into something wonderful. Today he has his own record label and recording studio and the respect of a great number of people in Dallas. He can teach himself how to do almost anything. He taught himself how to record his music. Then how to record his friends' music. Then how to mix and master (which is usually the work of three separate people!). Then he taught himself how to become a videographer, an editor, and a polymath.

From a young age, I had an idea of our money problems, and I had a sense of the ways in which money could change things for you. I was fifteen when I got my first job, and I used most of the money I earned to help pay for utilities and rent. But even so, my mom and brother and I spent part of my senior year living in one motel room. It was a chaotic environment for a kid to grow up in, and for a long time in my twenties and early thirties, I was a chaotic adult. Over time, though, I think the resilience I learned as a child and teenager helped me grow into someone who can handle chaos and remain still. Even in the worst situations, I can maintain a level of calmness and clarity while I work out what to do next.

One of the most crucial things I learned while growing up was how to use humor to diffuse situations and to keep upbeat in down times. For example, one time when I was a teenager, my mom and I were walking around the Richardson Square Mall in Dallas. We were in Dillard's looking for a watch or perfume or something. I can't quite recall the details, but I know it was something expensive, and we were either window shopping with the intention to save up for it or we had already done the saving and wanted to choose our purchase carefully. We walked up to the jewelry and perfume section, where a White woman was working behind the counter. She was on the phone with someone, and as she spoke to the other person, she gave us the once-over look up and down that we were so used to. Her body language was stuck up and standoffish, and it was clear that the second she saw us, she had already decided we were not worth her time. It was embarrassing and degrading to be dismissed in that way, and unfortunately, it was nothing new. Then we heard her exclaim loudly, in a very upper-crust, blue-blood voice, to the person on the other end of the line, "Yes, well, it's *San Sebastian*. We'll just ask *San Sebastian*."

My mom and I walked away, and as we headed back into the mall, we turned on our best high-society voices and couldn't stop saying to each other, "Oh, we'll just have *San Sebastian* get it. We'll get *San Sebastian* on the line." And so, as we did most of the time when we found ourselves in a situation that was embarrassing or uncomfortable or rough, we used humor to get past it and deal with it. Not only that: what started as a silly back-and-forth to mimic that ridiculous woman ended up being an inside joke that we still use more than twenty years later. Sometimes, just for fun, I'll call her "San Sebastian" or leave it as a little Easter egg in an Instagram post about her. And sometimes she'll text me those two words out of the blue, just as a way of saying hi, of connecting. Eventually, "San Sebastian" became our own private symbol of fanciness, of something happening that was very sophisticated.

For instance, ten years later, if I got a gig and I knew I was going to be on the road and get paid for a few weeks, I'd call up my mom or send her a text saying "San Sebastian has some good news. San Sebastian got me a job with this artist." Or if we got a tax refund or some sort of windfall that we weren't expecting, we said it was because San Sebastian had pulled some strings.

San Sebastian became a friend of ours that no one had met and no one understood; he was like the Charlie to our Angels. You never saw him. You didn't know where he was, who he was, how he had made his fortune, but to us, he was and still is the embodiment of success. These days, talking about San Sebastian is one of the ways my mom and I bond and how we retain that same sense of humor in both good and bad circumstances.

IT'S ABOUT HOPE, IT'S ABOUT HUMOR, IT'S ABOUT HUMANITY.

We've been in a lot of "fancy" situations in the last few years, where we've visited the homes of millionaires or billionaires, or we've been to parties or conferences where I've been a keynote speaker or received an award, or we've been guests at galas and dinners where our hosts might have paid $100,000 for the table (gasp!), and we still say, "San Sebastian brought us here." Every so often, I send my mom a birthday card or gift signed "San Sebastian." To me, it's about hope, it's about humor, it's about humanity, and it always had this tinge of "We'll get there."

One day I will buy a boat or a house for my mom, and I think you know what I'll call it.

11

The Best Music Comes from the Worst Breakups

n 2006, I was in a deep depression. I'd lost two things that were incredibly important to me: my magazine and my relationship. I was living in El Cajon, a suburb of San Diego, and I was around twenty-five years old. I had been dating my girlfriend for nearly three years at that point; we'd met online on Planet Out, which was a popular LGBTQ dating website (and a "start-up" before I knew what that was!). Megan Smith, the former chief technology officer of the United States under President Barack Obama (and the first female CTO) had once been the CEO of Planet Out. I'd go on to meet and become friends with Megan years later after starting Backstage. It still astonishes me how worlds can be so interconnected if you just pay attention.

I met that particular girlfriend on Planet Out when I was twenty-two. It wasn't my first relationship, but it was my first adult relationship. We got along so well, and we really cared about each other. I moved to San Diego from where I was staying at the time in Mississippi to be with her. She lived with her mother in a really expensive neighborhood north of San Diego, but a few months after we started dating, she moved in with me, in a . . . not-so-expensive neighborhood. She was two or three years younger than I was and in college. I didn't expect our relationship to last forever, but I definitely thought it was going better than it was when it ended. I found out she had cheated on me with a younger friend of hers, whom I'd recently taken to International House of Pancakes to help counsel her through her relationship problems. Ha! Can you believe it? The fact that I'd been helping that chick, who knew at the time that she and my long-term girlfriend had cheated on me, was a real blow. I think I even paid for the meal. Believe it or not, that would be only the first of two times I was involved in lesbian drama at an IHOP in my twenties. But I digress.

I learned that my girlfriend had also become involved in some extracurricular activities with an all-lesbian sorority at college. That was a lot to learn about all at once. And although today I find humor in the fact that it reads like an inmate origin story from *Orange Is the New Black,* I was heartbroken at the time.

Around the same time, my magazine, *Interlude,* had gone under for the first time. It went under twice, but the first time was during the same time period that I learned my live-in girlfriend had been cheating on me with multiple people (how did those young women get *anything* done at school? I wondered). So it was a lot to deal with. I was super depressed, drinking a lot of Trader Joe's "Two-Buck Chuck" (cheap yet effective wine with its own mythology stemming from a broken relationship), and spending a lot of time on the interwebs, talking to friends and drowning my sorrows.

One day I remember looking at a pile of clothes that my ex

had left in my apartment and thinking, "I want to throw these clothes down the stairs. I want to light them on fire, throw them down the stairs, and watch them burn. Or better yet, I want to sell them all or put them all outside and let the neighborhood kids take their favorites." They were expensive items, thigh-high boots and designer-label clothing, because she was from an affluent family and had a lot of nice things. I remember thinking in a drunken stupor, "Man, it would be really fantastic right now to watch this burn to ashes on the stairs."

But I stopped myself and said, "No, because then that's only more mess for me to clean up." She'd already left a mess for me to clean up emotionally, and I was tired. I didn't want to clean up anymore. So I decided against that and instead went onto MySpace. That was right when YouTube was getting popular, and MySpace had started a feature where you could embed videos in posts. I decided I would find some random video that had something to do with lesbians or was about two women in a relationship. Remember, this was, as they say, "back in the day." We didn't have your newfangled Netflix yet, and *The L Word* was just a baby itself, so when you went through a nasty "lesbian" breakup, you had to search and type and exert all kinds of energy looking for ways to commiserate with others.

The idea was that I was going to post the video and just write my immediate thoughts about it, just as a way to entertain myself, keep myself sane, keep myself sharp, and mostly have something to do because I was going crazy not being productive. I felt as though that would create some sort of connection to the few people who were paying attention at the time. Plus it was a way to find the snark in a bad situation, which always helped lift my spirits.

So I posted my first blog. I don't remember what the video

was or what I said to accompany it, but I do remember that it got a lot of likes (or whatever the equivalent of likes was back then). A lot of people saw it, more people then followed me. I thought, "Wow, that's really cool and strange that people are seeing this." So I kept going, started getting comments and interacting with people, and that cheered me up. Some of the things that I posted were funny; some were snarky because I was in a really pissed-off mood. Some were heartbreaking because I was sad and lonely, and some were informational just because, why not? No matter which kind of post it was, I was getting interaction. For me it was like an awakening; I now understood how online interaction could work with multiple people rather than one-on-one. It was one of the first times I realized that people were paying attention to what I had to say. Some of those people had been fans of the first iteration of my magazine (an indie music vibe with the likes of My Chemical Romance, All-American Rejects, and Jenny Lewis on the cover). A lot of them were friends whom I had either known beforehand or had picked up online, but most of them were strangers I hadn't known prior to this, which meant they were reacting to something they enjoyed in the writing or the clip.

I didn't understand it right away, but it's very clear today that those were some of the foundational moments not only in social media but in starting a movement. That messy breakup and the days that followed turned out to be a master class in scale, impact, reach, niche, and authenticity.

A few posts in, I had gotten so many responses and so many messages about it that I thought, "This could actually stand alone. This is something that has its own life and its own merit. What's more, I'm enjoying it." Finding joy in a time when it felt like my whole life was falling apart around me was so clutch. It might have saved me from going down an extremely dark path.

So I decided to start blogging. I did a couple of Google searches to figure out how to start a blog and what HTML was, and then I opened a Blogspot account. I called the blog *Your Daily Lesbian Moment!* I wanted it to be daily because I thought the "daily" would get people's attention and keep them coming back for updates. I also thought the title was provocative and would create curiosity. I didn't always post daily, but people certainly visited daily. I went on to post more than a thousand times between 2006 and 2012.

The work got more intricate and complex over time as the blog became more popular and more people shared the posts. I had my own brand of snark, relatability, and earnestness, and I was giving my point of view of pop culture as a lesbian. To give you an idea of the content, one of my most popular posts was titled "Top 20 Movies You Watched as a Kid . . . 'Cause You Were a Lesbian." I went on to list movies such as *My Girl* ('cause, duh) and describe why watching one Ninja Turtle movie meant you were a good big sister to a brother but watching all three meant you were a raging homosexual. Watching more than one indie film starring Angelina Jolie pre–Lara Croft *and* knowing all the lines to *Set It Off?* Ma'am, there's something I need to tell you.

One of the coolest parts of writing the blog back then in the pre-Twitter world was that if something happened that was topical, I could write about it and within minutes I would have it online. People came back to the site to see what content I'd posted that day or week or month and what I had to say about the latest in pop culture and lesbian culture. People started messaging me at eight in the morning, asking where my daily post was because they were so excited to see it. It was a bit like that episode of *Friends* where Monica starts making candy for the neighbors and soon they come back looking for their fix.

Over the six or so years that I ran the blog, there were two features that were really popular. The first one was called "Your Daily Lesbian," and it was a series of posts that profiled readers of the site. Somewhere along the line I figured out that there were a lot of women who liked women checking out this blog and some of them might be looking for friends, dates, or partners but either weren't the online dating type or lived in cities and towns where they couldn't hang out with hundreds of like-minded women each weekend as I could in California. The main age demographic that came to the site was sixteen to thirty-five years old. The feature was eighteen-plus because it was used as a kind of matchmaking service. I started it by asking "Hey, do you want to be featured on the site? Thousands of people are looking at this blog. Tell me your name, age, and location and give me a blurb and a photograph and I'll put it on the site." I started doing that, and people started meeting one another. They were already meeting each other in the comments or in the MySpace posts and on Facebook when I later migrated there. So this was a natural extension of that, with more intention and purpose.

I have no way of keeping count of exactly how many friendships were forged or exactly how many couples got together and even got married, but it was in the hundreds of couples and matches made. I received emails and DMs weekly for years letting me know that I'd somehow helped someone either meet an important person in her life or, in some cases, stopped her from taking her own life because she no longer felt alone and hopeless in the world for being gay/queer.

The romantic matchmaking aspect of it became so popular that around 2009 I launched a beta matchmaking site called Juliet and Juliet. The name was crowdsourced, which I liked, and I was really impressed with it. Years later when I would learn more about tech start-ups and want to start my own, that idea would be the one I'd almost create. Life had other plans, and instead I launched Backstage Capital. But you can see why it was a tough decision at first.

Another popular feature of the blog was my commentary on the TV series *The L Word*. I did a weekly top ten list of that week's episode. At that time, *The L Word,* for women who liked women, was revolutionary. For those of us who had grown up in places where we had to be in the closet and those of us who still felt we had to be closeted in certain situations, we were seeing ourselves (or at least a luxury version of ourselves) on TV for the first time. We had a lot of fun with *The L Word,* and *The L Word* took a lot of our abuse because we felt like it belonged to us.

It was sort of like our sports team. Your favorite sports team—you love them, you have your favorite team members and you'll ride or die for them, you go to all of their games, you watch what you can, you wear the shirt. But you do get angry at some of the decisions they make, some of the calls the coaches make or some of the plays, and you yell at the TV because you know they can do better! That's how I, and millions of us, treated *The L Word*. We loved it and it frustrated us at the same time.

So I would post my thoughts on it, usually with a lot of irreverence. The running theme was that I was deeply in love with Rachel Shelley, who played Helena Peabody, the posh British vixen who is rich and powerful. I talked about that almost every week. I actually met Rachel Shelley at my first Dinah Shore Weekend, a Palm Springs gathering of ten thousand women who like women that resembles Florida's spring break. I didn't know she was going to be there, and as she walked by me in all of her glory, all I could muster to whisper-mutter was "I can die happy now." She stopped and looked at me, laughed a bit, gave me a wink as though we were in *Weird Science* (the number one movie on my "you know you're a lesbian if . . ." movie list, BTW), and carried on into the sunset.

I also talked about decisions that were made about Shane's hair (that topic was extremely important and still wakes me up in the middle of the night at times) or plotlines that didn't make much sense to me, and I gave each of the ten topics a punny title. People flocked to that particular post every week, and it was the most popular section of my website for years.

Sometimes I got warnings from Blogspot about the content on my site, and I would have to argue against the idea that it was pornographic. I used the blog to talk about relationships, and that did include sex, and I was also pretty open and body/sex positive. The point was to normalize the representation of our lives in its many shades and nuances—including sex—so that the thousands of women who had been made to feel "wrong" or "sinful" would know they were not alone and were not "bad." So none of it was meant to be pornographic; it was meant to be entertaining, relatable, and informative. I was talking to a subculture, to my subculture, about the normal parts of our lives. Things have improved since then, but at the time a photo of two women kissing was considered explicit content, especially if it was accessed in a public place such as a library or on a school computer. Even a completely innocuous website that included any kind of information about LGBTQ+ issues could be flagged for explicit content, so the fact that I put "lesbian" into the name didn't make it easy for me.

Occasionally I would visit a different city and I'd be approached by women, and sometimes men, who would ask for a photograph and want to hang out or buy me a drink because they read the blog. I would be invited to go to *The L Word* fan screenings. I wrote for the SuicideGirls website and for AOL's now-defunct LGBT blog called *Queer Sighted,* and I was featured in some magazines, such as *Curve.* A common theme you've probably caught on to by now is that I've always wanted to foster connection. Though starting the blog came from heartbreak, maintaining it was fueled by the same feeling that had me wearing six watches in the third grade, starting an indie music magazine, or touring the country in an old van with Norwegian rockers.

When I migrated the blog to Facebook, it was an entirely new and fresh thing, because now there were people who were able to really connect, and I could forge relationships, talk to people, and meet people in real life. I would post a personal missive and get dozens of replies within moments. It was something else; it was special. It's almost surreal, looking back, that it was such an intense, huge part of my life. One thing I do regret is that I never turned the blog into an email newsletter, which I think would have done really well. I regret not having kept a proper email list, because when I moved from MySpace I had about fifty thousand followers. And then MySpace died, so I moved over to Facebook after the recommendation of my really good friend Sarah Smith. It was a great decision because MySpace became a parking lot, but then I had "only" about five thousand followers on Facebook. So first I lost all of the social equity that I had built and earned over time when I migrated from MySpace to Facebook, and then I lost it again when I stopped using Facebook on a daily basis a few years after that.

The blog slowed down because life got in the way. People got older, I got older, and the way I used online social networks changed. But if I had had that mailing list from MySpace or a mailing list from Facebook, it could have all traveled with me. I definitely feel like shouting from the rooftops that if you have any sort of following, if anyone is keeping track of what you're doing, if you have a presence on Instagram or Twitter today or a presence anywhere, whatever is hot right now when you're reading this, make an email list! Email has been tried and true for the past twenty years. If I can encourage you to take anything away from this chapter, it's to start an email list today. Email has stood the test of time and most likely will continue to do so for at least the foreseeable future.

A few years later I would go on to create a popular Twitter profile called Modern L Word, inspired by the fanfic Twitter account Modern Seinfeld. I set the premise "What would it be like if *The L Word* were on in 2013, 2014 and '15" and so on. After having been dormant for three or four years in that world, that really stirred me again. And believe it or not, the Modern L Word Twitter account started days after I had the worst breakup of my life. So in a lot of ways I'm like one of your favorite musicians: my best music comes from the worst breakups.

Resilience is something that you will always need. It will help you get through the toughest parts of life, and no matter how successful you are, there will always be tough parts. Resilience is not how you feel in the moment when something happens, but how you continue afterward.

Your Daily Lesbian Moment! was created out of moments of sadness and anger at my situation. None of that would have happened had I not been going through a terrible breakup, the failure of my business, utter heartbreak, and depression. In my lowest moments I wanted revenge for the way I had been treated by my girlfriend. But instead of wasting that energy on revenge or anger or bitterness, I channeled it into something positive. This is something I would recommend to everyone; use the energy that anger gives you to create something new or to get your house in order. Repurpose it. The next time you feel as though everything is broken, as though you have nothing to give, get creative.

12

Shane Is My Homegirl

Overall, *Your Daily Lesbian Moment!* was one of the best parts of my adult life. Writing the blog was always fulfilling for me. I never dreaded doing it; it was always exciting, and I felt very much in control of it. As my readership grew, I began to add advertising links to the website. I knew only the slightest amount of HTML, but it was enough to embed photos at the side of my blog posts with links to advertisers' websites. That was where most of the revenue came from; I would charge between $30 and $1,000 for advertising space, depending on what the company was selling. When my blog was in its prime, I had an average of fifty thousand unique visitors each month according to Google analytics. That held steady for two or three years. The most I ever made from advertising in one month was probably around $1,500, which wasn't too shabby.

I remember learning that some LGBTQ bloggers I was friendly with were making $6,000 a month from *one (!)* of their ad spots on their popular website. I would have to have ten times the number of readers to accomplish that, so I definitely tried to increase my readership many times. But after a few years I understood that the fifty thousand readers I had developed a relationship with were more valuable than having half a million, even if it meant I'd never make "passive income" from the site.

It was interesting to track the advertising and merchandise sales. It gave me something of an education in sales, and I made notes on it from month to month. I also had Amazon affiliate links, which meant I could promote things personally. That worked well for me because my readers were very engaged. They would come back to the site up to twenty times a month, so they would see the advertisement multiple times. They also trusted my taste and my judgment, which is really important if you're trying to sell someone else's products.

I made the most revenue on the site from merchandise. I sold T-shirts that said things such as I'D GO GAY FOR ANGELINA or WHO KILLED JENNY or SHANE IS MY HOMEGIRL/HOMOGIRL. Over a six-year period, I sold thousands of shirts. That generated a lot of revenue but not a lot of profit. I would come up with ideas for T-shirts and either have them printed and shipped to me and then mail them out or have them printed at an on-demand printing shop. Most of the time I was having them printed, sitting at home surrounded by boxes of shirts, and sending them out to customers myself, handwriting up to four hundred address labels a month. I usually gave each shirt a limited amount of sales time, so I would promote it in a post, add it to the advertisement side of the blog with a "Buy Now" button that linked to my PayPal account, and then let readers know how long it would be available.

Eventually I got smart and started printing people's addresses, but I was still hand folding the shirts, packaging them, and going to the post office to send them out. In my prime of doing that, I could look at someone wearing a shirt and tell what size it was. I could go to a concert at a club, pick up a shirt, and know immediately which one would fit a given person. It became second nature to me, as though I were the Rain Man of Fruit of the Loom. I'd also slung a few shirts in my days as an indie tour manager. When you're managing the tour of an independent band or artist, you're not just the tour manager, you're the booker, you're the van driver, you're the roadie, you're the production manager, you're the merch seller. Selling merchandise before, during, and after artists' sets gave me a lot of information about selling to people one-on-one. I gained a lot from talking to people about the products. Most of the time it was a good conversation. I was making someone happy because I was delivering something they wanted, and they let me know how excited they were, or we made a friendly exchange because the shirt they got wasn't exactly what they wanted. I got market research from thousands and thousands of customers over the years.

This is another example of my not really understanding unit economics back then, because I should have made a lot of money from it. But I tended to undercut myself, undersell myself, and not charge the right amount. I had the best intentions, a product people loved, a loyal fan base, but I would run out of capital or not optimize for profit because I didn't know any better. I always optimized for connecting with people and being accessible; I thought I would rather have one thousand people wear one of my shirts and get joy from that product than have only one hundred wear it at a higher price. To me it was more about how many people could be involved rather than making economic sense, and that's something that has followed me my entire life. It resurfaced when I brought the magazine back for the second time, and it has resurfaced when I've attempted other things. Today I let founders know that I've been there and I know it's not always easy to figure that out. So when I say, "be the money," that means know your numbers, do your market research, make sure your unit economics work and make sense, all of that. I am saying it from a place of wanting you not to repeat the mistakes I've made. Talk to people who have been there, done that, before attempting something new. It's always worth the time investment.

> YOU HAVE TO LOOK AT
> YOUR EXPERIENCES AND
> UNDERSTAND THEM FOR
> WHAT THEY ARE:
> AN EDUCATION BUILT
> JUST FOR YOU.

Selling merch didn't always go as planned, best intentions or not. Sometimes I'd send out the wrong shirt, or, even worse, sometimes the shirt got lost in the mail or was delayed weeks or months because my cash flow wasn't on point. That happened only 2 or 3 percent of the time, but when you add it up, it was a lot. Sometimes I would get the angriest emails or even phone calls. People would leave messages on my personal line or email me, cursing me out, telling me I was a horrible person. I remember one time a guy called me from Australia and yelled obscenities at me for what seemed like a solid, unrelenting five minutes because the hoodie he had ordered for his wife—ahem—had not made it to him in weeks. There was a ton to unpack there, but again, I digress. I couldn't do anything but say "I'm really sorry" repeatedly, and I think I cried afterward. I learned a lot from that; I never, ever wanted it to happen, and I took it very seriously when it did. Sometimes it was "just" a shirt, and sometimes it was thousands of dollars worth of merchandise, like the time I couldn't deliver my magazines on time. Some of those times were the toughest of my life; I hated that some people never received their products. Even though thousands did, it was the dozens who didn't that kept me up at night. I can't be too mad about what happened, though. You have to look at your experiences and understand them for what they are: an education built just for you. It was such a unique position to be in, especially at that time, and being able to reach so many people made the hard times feel worth it.

As I went on to learn more and more about start-ups and entrepreneurship in general, I realized that many of my previous experiences were incredibly common for people who build and are entrepreneurs. You'll meet some people who are unscrupulous, and they do not represent the entrepreneur I'm talking about. I'm talking about you, the person who has maybe felt a bit different from your peers, who is always thinking of new ideas and, unlike the majority of the world, attempts to execute many of them. This can be a lonely type of personality. But when I'm feeling my lowest or loneliest as an entrepreneur, I think of people such as Richard Branson, Janet Jackson, Ani DiFranco, and many of the hundreds of founders I have invested in who faced seemingly insurmountable odds. Because of their perseverance and unflappable resolve, they have risen from the ashes time and time again.

13

Forgiveness Is a Productivity Hack

Disappointment is something I have encountered frequently since I founded Backstage Capital, and I want to talk about that, because it's not always something that someone in this business shares. We're encouraged to give the impression that everything is happening as it should be, success after success, but so much happens behind closed doors as part of running a business. The way I built the firm and in the industry itself, where you are counting on investments and handshakes—er, fist bumps— and your ability to convince others to see the dream, there are a lot of unfulfilled expectations and letdowns. Throughout the process of starting and running Backstage Capital, there have been many times—and when I say many, I mean more than a hundred—when I thought I had secured an investment into the fund and then it didn't happen. In a venture fund business model that depends on securing pots of money, the loss of an expected investment can be devastating. It was with very little irony that I called our firm's podcast *The Boot-strapped VC.*

I'll give you an example: there was an angel investor who told me they would commit to investing $100,000 in Back-stage Capital's second fund, a circa $1.2 million vehicle. At that point in the life of the company, that amount of money would have been nearly 10 percent of the fund and would have been invested over the course of an entire year. It would have been the investment money for two to four separate companies. And each of those companies would have required the small Backstage team and I to take time to nurture the deal and carry out our due diligence. After a few weeks of talking to the angel investor, answering questions, taking phone calls and in-person meetings, getting a yes, and send-ing our wire information and legal documents through . . . they changed their mind. On the day of the expected transac-tion, the day the $100,000 that we had been counting on and expecting was meant to arrive, the person emailed me and said that unfortunately their circumstances had changed. They were no longer in a financial position to execute on the commitment made, and there was really nothing either of us could do about it.

Similar situations have occurred where investors had un-expected changes to their personal circumstances, changed their minds, didn't feel the same way they had felt when they promised the money, or simply ghosted. It's happened to Backstage at least a dozen times between 2015 and 2019, when the amount was in the $50,000 to $5 million range. It's not always someone being cruel or intentionally harmful, but it does always have a severe impact on a fledgling company such as Backstage.

When a company, family, institutional investor, or individual is investing a lot of money in your investment fund, they do what is called "due diligence." Depending on the size of the investment and the size and stage of your fund, this can take months or even years. There are many rounds of phone calls, meetings, and interviews, similar to what happens in fundraising rounds for individual start-ups, although the fundraising cycle for a fund can be two to ten times as long as a start-up's. The investors talk to multiple people in your network, including other investors, companies you've worked with and invested in, companies you've said no to, employees both past and present, those who have invested in you, and others in the ecosystem whom they deem relevant to your particular thesis and status. They will interview them and have multiple rounds of meetings. They'll pore through your finances, create spreadsheets and projections, do data analysis, and construct an internal "deal memo" that is passed around and reviewed by multiple decision makers. The larger the organization, the more detailed this process can be. But even with individual limited partners (LPs) or family offices, that can be quite an ordeal.

It can feel as though it's taking forever—which makes sense, because we're talking about a lot of money. But we've been through this deep due diligence with LPs who are talking about investing $25,000 or more, and we have nearly two hundred investors. Figure that each "yes" took at least nine nos (and in most cases, many more than that), and we're talking about thousands of conversations. So imagine the toll this has taken over time, and imagine what happens when you finally get a "yes" and it is taken away in a puff of smoke. When someone's mind changes in the last hour, someone's liquidity has changed, or someone's concerns about our risks have been compounded by time, circumstances, or risk aversion, it's deeply disappointing!

We even had one case when we were closing in on a final commitment from a company to invest millions of dollars in us, which would have carried us for years, but the investor was arrested before we were able to close on the deal. I mean, that feels plucked right out of a storyline on my favorite TV show, *General Hospital*. But alas, it was real life.

At least three times, we've had deals that involved millions of dollars promised or alluded to that didn't come through. It's been incredibly impactful not having this money and very surprising in each case. But the documents were not signed yet, so there was really no recourse.

Those were disappointments that I just had to live with. I knew it internally but couldn't or wouldn't share it with the world because I knew we'd need to be strategic. You can't burn bridges no matter how you're feeling in the moment, and you also need to play five-dimensional chess when it comes to how your words and actions will affect others you care about. In all those cases when money didn't come through, some or all of it was due to go to someone else: an underestimated founder and their team, a vendor, our crew's salaries. That's an incredible amount of pressure, an incredible amount of responsibility, and the disappointment can feel crushing at times. So the last thing I want to do is go on Twitter and call someone out for not following through on an investment, only to have them retaliate against one of our stakeholders or not invest in the next underrepresented founder.

Over the years, I've learned how to adapt very quickly, to compartmentalize to protect myself, and how to separate the personal from the professional. This is not something that you learn once and you are great at it forever. You have to work on this as you would a muscle. You have to work on this as a craft. You have to be able to take in what has happened, accept it as reality, and convince yourself that it will be okay, that it is not the end, because a lot of these bigger moments can feel like everything in the moment. They can feel like the end of something. There's a mourning period that can come from it, and over the past few years I have found myself mourning a lot of things that I thought were going to happen, mourning lost futures. But I know I am doing this for something much bigger than myself, and it is too important to get this right for me to buckle under the pressures of such disappointments.

Silicon Valley Bank economist Natalie Fratto has coined the term "adaptability quotient" (AQ) to go along with the better-known intelligence quotient (IQ) and emotional quotient (EQ). She has often used me as a case study in fleshing out her thesis around adaptability being the largest indicator of someone's future success, and she wrote about me in a 2018 think piece called "Is Silicon Valley Over? Not If Investors Can Adapt":[*]

> Arlan Hamilton, Founder of Backstage Capital, is a Black, queer, female VC poised to succeed because of her high AQ. Individually, she's had to exhibit adaptability many times over—she's navigated homelessness, succeeded in a music career, and pivoted to raise a seed fund when every statistic was against her. As an

---

[*]   https://hackernoon.com/is-silicon-valley-over-not-if-investors-can
      -adapt-505f0b61e53b.

investor, she's capitalizing on that unique point of view by investing in founders like herself—a group that traditional investors are widely neglecting. With her first fund, Arlan plans to capture future value by investing in 100 companies that are led by underrepresented founders, with half being women of color.

When it comes to Silicon Valley, we talk a lot about the positives and the highlights and the glory of it all—the glory of what Backstage gets to do and what our whole ecosystem can do. But we all know that there's a lot more disappointment than glory. When you have audacious plans and goals, when your ambition is matched only by the brightness of the sun, you are signing up for a great deal of emotional extremes that you must learn to bear.

I think the key is not to isolate yourself. It can feel as though you're the only one experiencing this emotion, but disappointment is extremely relatable. It doesn't matter what the disappointment is, whether it's monetary, tangible, an experience that you're missing out on, or a disappointment in someone's behavior. Everyone has experienced it and probably experiences it in some form regularly. You can't control what happens to you or around you, and you can't control your circumstances. You cannot control whether a rich person says yes or no to you (oh, how I've tried, y'all). But you *can* do your best to showcase what you have, make the case for it, and pitch it. You can do your best to be on time, be professional, be open to constructive criticism, answer questions, know your stuff. You cannot control another person's decision, circumstances, or bank account. You can't stop someone from ghosting you.

What you can control is how you handle it. Especially if

you're a leader, if you isolate yourself, if you put yourself into an emotional prison because you feel the pressure on you from all sides, you'll suffocate. I've had to learn as best I can to let it go. Disappointment is tough, but holding on to it and clinching the feeling in your chest, carrying it around with you indefinitely, will only make matters worse. Obsessing over the future you'd imagined and lost and spinning out of control in your mind about why something didn't happen is a waste of time, energy, and fight. And you need all of those to move on and work out what the next step should be.

FORGIVENESS IS THE ULTIMATE PRODUCTIVITY HACK.

I talk a lot about repurposing one emotion for something else. Repurposing fear into energy and excitement, repurposing anger into action. Something that has made the most impact on me is realizing that forgiveness is the ultimate productivity hack.

Part of what I've had to teach myself over the past few years is how to let go of disappointment. In order to recover from it, you have to be alert, awake, aware. You can't be any of those things if you're hunched over in sorrow because something didn't work out. There's no prescription of how long it should take you to get over it. There's not even anything that says you *should* get over it. But there has to be something that kicks in, a different gear that you shift into when you are incredibly disappointed and when life hands you circumstances that are seemingly overwhelming. You have to turn a gear inside you that enables you to take one more step forward and not get lost and buried in your own sorrow. This is how I've gone from the places I've been to where I am now. Know your value, and do not let anyone treat you poorly. Do not accept abuse. But also understand the power that comes in controlling how much you let anger and disappointment overwhelm you. Imagine transforming the feeling of losing love, suffering from a breaking heart, or being told the morning of a big wire that it's not coming in after all into power and productivity. You've just taken back control of the situation.

14

On Level Ground You Will Excel

When I was in the fifth grade, my school told my mom I had to learn to swim. It was a safety thing. I grew up in Texas, and there were a lot of homes with pools. There was some rule where all the kids had to know how to swim for safety, and I was one of the few kids who didn't know how to swim. There was a class at a nearby high school that had its own pool. For some reason, I can't remember why, I started the class late. I think it was a weeklong class, and I started it a day or two later than everyone else. I was already worried because I had to wear a swimsuit and I had self-image issues. I knew my hair was going to get wet and puffy; I hadn't started getting it done at a salon yet because I was so young. Most important though, I was *really* afraid of the water.

When I was much, much younger, my mom had taken me to YMCA swimming classes. The instructor had thought it was a good idea to hold me underwater longer than I wanted. That terrified me, and I never went back. I was afraid of drowning or of getting water in my lungs, or of panicking and not being able to get out. I was taller and heavier than everyone else. In my ten-year old mind, I thought I was too heavy to swim and I'd sink to the bottom of the pool. No matter how you sliced it, I thought I was going to make a scene.

I joined the class. The instructor explained how swimming worked, and I had a pair of goggles so that when I went underwater, I could see. Once I'd gotten over the initial trepidation of immersing my hair, I dunked my head underwater and opened my eyes, and realized I liked it. It was refreshing and fun, and I felt athletic in a way I hadn't before. I understood it. It was logical to me, the different strokes and movements. I also understood that for the first time, my height was going to be an advantage. I could swim faster because my arms and legs were longer, and my weight wasn't a problem because I was buoyed by the water. What? Awesome.

At the end of the week, we had a race to see who could swim to the other end of the pool and back the fastest. On your mark, get set, *go*! And guess what? I won it. I started the class with the least amount of experience because I was late to it and scared senseless, and by the end of it, once I knew the rules and got my bearings, I was faster than the rest of the class. I think about this whenever I'm worried that I'm too far behind or that I don't belong in a certain circle because I don't have the same set of qualifications or expertise. Given the opportunity, I can succeed, even when I'm scared out of my mind.

In the summer of 2017, I was invited to a retreat in the French Alps by one of our larger LPs in our first fund. It held an annual retreat to which it would invite several of its portfolio companies to meet and talk about the future of finance.

Founders came from all over the world; the retreat brought a lot of brilliant minds to one spot. I accepted the invitation.

It was without doubt one of the most beautiful and serene places I'd ever visited. My hotel was located at the bottom of a large incline; if you needed to get anywhere, you had to walk up a mountain or hill to get to the point where you could take a vehicle.

One of the days I was there, I needed to go to a meeting that had been arranged at the top of one of these hills on the side of a mountain. Yodel-ay-hee-hoo! I found myself walking with about twelve other people, all heading to the meeting up a steep incline. I was the heaviest person there, probably the least fit. I'm also very top-heavy, so it was harder to breathe, and as a result of all that, I was at the very back of the pack.

Not only was the hill steep (perhaps a sixty-degree incline), but we were already around 15,000 feet above sea level and the high altitude made breathing even more difficult. I was out of breath just climbing the hill but with people ahead of me. I remember thinking, "This is an analogy of my life." In that moment I reflected on it: there were people all around me, passing me, getting to places faster than I was. They were heading to the same destination as I was but getting there more easily, with less angst and pain. I wondered if the strapping young men at the front of the pack thought they were somehow better, smarter, superior in some way because they were able to get to the top faster?

I was the heaviest person, so I had the most weight to carry up the hill. I was the least fit, so I had the worst lung capacity, and it was the hardest for me to breathe, as far as I know. Most of the people around me were men, so they didn't have to be aware of their breasts pushing down against their lungs. I had a lot of time to think about that on the long, strenuous walk. This self-reflection and life observation is something I do daily in almost every situation, even then, when I could barely breathe and all I wanted to do was roll my way back down that hill and take a nap wherever I landed. I can't help myself.

When we got to the top, something interesting happened. We were on a level field. We were no longer at an incline. We were all able to walk at the same pace. I noticed I started walking faster, I started breathing easier, and I finally made it. I thought about how in life and in business, I feel as though I'm on that hill quite often. I feel as though it's taken me much longer to get to the top, but once I'm there, I exceed and excel. What I aim to do with Backstage Capital is put underestimated founders on that level playing field. Given the same opportunities, they can also walk with those hugely successful founders. When you're underestimated, sometimes it can feel as though you're at the bottom of the mountain while everyone else has tickets for the ski lift. I want to give everyone a ticket; even if they don't succeed, they deserve to see the view from the top of the mountain. They deserve a chance.

PART IV

AUTHENTICITY

15

Unapologetic Authenticity

Being so deeply truly yourself,
as a nonnegotiable, is the answer to everything.

'␣ve found, both throughout my career and in my personal
life, that authenticity is of the utmost importance. Anytime
I've tried to stray away from who I am, it's come back to
haunt me. Being 100 percent yourself is simultaneously the
easiest and the hardest thing you can do. On the one hand, you
get to go with your gut and do what feels right; you don't have
to put on a performance, and when people like you, you know
it's for you. On the other, the world is constantly telling us to
change ourselves. We're always being pushed to make ourselves more palatable to the outside world, make ourselves
smaller so we fit into the small boxes of expectation that society throws at us. When your gender, race, sexuality, ability, or
any other characteristic is othered, is already read as "different," being yourself can be a radical act.

When I was still very young, my mother became a Jehovah's Witness, so I was brought up in religion. I learned to read very early for my age, as it was important to the Witnesses that you be able to study the Bible as early as possible. On weekends my mother, my brother, and I spent our time knocking on doors and talking to people about religion. I ultimately didn't agree with the Witnesses and left as a teenager. To say that I do not condone their messages or actions is an understatement, and I have publicly stated my distaste for the organization.

Being a Witness taught me from a very early age to get used to having doors slammed in my face. Being a Witness definitely made me an outsider at school. If there are two things that kids love, they are birthdays and Christmas. I still have trouble remembering my best friends' birthdays now, because I spent so many years not celebrating. I wasn't proud to be a Witness, but at the same time, I didn't want other kids making fun of me or my family. It was one of those "I can be negative about it, but you can't" situations; there was an element of dignity that I needed to retain on behalf of my family. I also understand today what I couldn't then, which is that I have a strong sense of justice when it comes to freedom of religion, speech, and expression, and defending our family's rights to all three of these was at the base of my objection to any mean feedback from other kids.

As well as reading, I had been taught my multiplication tables early by my mom. She thought it was really important that I knew how to add and multiply and subtract and all of that early. So my arithmetic and reading levels were high when I started elementary school. When I was in the first grade, I was taught by Miss Hurson, who was one of my favorite teachers ever. We used to play a math game called

"Around the World." She had a piece of paper hanging on the wall with all of our names on it, and if you won a game of "Around the World," you got a star sticker next to your name. The game worked like this: Miss Hurson would choose one student to start off the game. The student would start the game by standing behind another student while they sat at their desk. Miss Hurson would hold up a very large index card with a multiplication problem on it, and the two students, one standing and one sitting, would each try to work out the answer first. The first of the two students to call out the right answer would win that round and then get to go and stand behind the next student. You would do this as much as you could. You might win two or three rounds. You might say the right answer two or three times, and then someone else would beat you and you'd have to sit down.

On the rare occasion when someone made it all around the room, which was approximately twenty students, it was called "going around the world," and that person won the whole game. We'd play it only one day a week or so, and it was something I always looked forward to. Here's the thing: every time I played the game, I won. I had fun because it was challenging and I wanted to know what the next question was to see if I could get the answer right. I have also always had a competitive side that strove for excellence, so the game was thrilling to me even as mini me.

Eventually I won so often that Miss Hurson had to create a new rule that I could win only once a week. She didn't even mask it as "no one can win more than once a week"; it was specifically "Arlan can win only once a week" because I so dominated the playing field. After I had won once, I could not continue playing. Then, at some point, Miss Hurson would say, "Okay, we're going to just start with Arlan." I would get up, and I would go around the world, and I would win, and then I would get a star next to my name, and then I would have to sit out the rest of the game. While the rest of the kids were playing, I'd always know the answer in my head and say it to myself. At the time I thought it wasn't exactly fair and it disappointed me; I thought I was being punished for being good at something. It felt that way, but now I understand that it wasn't going to help any of the other students if I was dominating the score and the game.

By the end of the year, my name had so many star stickers next to it, they went across the piece of paper and onto the next line, and the next. Eventually I was put into a higher grade level, to third or fourth grade, to play in their game. I did okay. I held my own, although I didn't smoke them and become Bobby Fischer or anything. (For you young'uns, the Bobby Fischer reference would be like my referring to Sheldon from *The Big Bang Theory*.)

As I got older, school became harder. Not only did I find the other kids hard to relate to, it seemed that the teachers found me hard to relate to. The Georgetown Law Center on Poverty and Inequality published a study in 2017 about the problem of the "adultification" of Black girls in the United States. Titled "Girlhood Interrupted: The Erasure of Black Girls' Childhood," the study showed that adults view Black girls as less innocent, more independent, and older than they are. Black girls are felt to be less in need of nurturing, protection, and comfort and are assumed to know more about sex than White girls. The "adultification" process begins at age five. The report suggested that those perceptions "may contribute to *harsher punishment* by educators and school resource officers." Not only was I a Black girl, I was also very tall for my age and physically well developed. I was a bright student, getting As and Bs on my work, but I continually got Cs and Fs on behavior. I was, and still am, naturally very curious. I asked a lot of questions. Instead of nurturing that curiosity and helping me find the answers I was looking for, many of the teachers sent me to the principal's office, citing "disruption" as my offense. I ended up in trouble a lot, and it always felt unfair to me. I take much responsibility for learning that I could feel better about myself by cracking up a classroom with humor, so some of those trips were definitely well founded. But many—too many—were not.

I remember that in a tenth-grade journalism class we were reading the Starr Report about President Bill Clinton and we were asked by our teacher how we would feel if we were Hillary Clinton. Now, I would question why at that age we were reading a report that included graphic details of sexual acts, but that's another story altogether. I raised my hand and told the teacher that if I were Clinton's wife, I'd be "pissed." Now, remember, I grew up in a religious home and had a Black mother from the South, so you know I was already trained not to curse. I'd once seen a White friend curse in front of her mom and literally started writing her eulogy in my head immediately because I just knew she was going to get it. But she didn't. Point is, I did not think "pissed" was a curse word, and if I had, I would not have used it. The teacher sent me out into the hall as punishment for using the word. Now, during the same conversation, a White boy in my class said that Bill Clinton was "screwed,"—meaning he was in so much trouble—and he received exactly no punishment or reprimand. Things like that didn't make sense to me then, and they don't today.

In our social studies class, every student had to present on a current event. I always had questions about people's current events, and this was seen as my being disruptive. I could have learned from that that curiosity was a negative personality trait, that finding answers wasn't important and I should just accept what I was told and never question anything. Luckily, I didn't. Luckily, my mother was Earline Sims, and she'd taught me from day one that I was just as good as any other kid and to speak up for myself.

My brother, Alfred, had a difficult time in school, too. He struggled both with schoolwork and with the way he was treated. After a certain number of Fs, he dropped out of school in ninth grade. Alfred is smart. He's one of those people who loves to take things apart and put them together again, who can look at pictures of how something is built and do it without reading the instructions. What we didn't know back then was that Alfred is dyslexic and has ADD. He also struggles with anxiety. Had we known that at the time, he could have been given the help he needed to reach his full potential in education, but no one considered that they might be underestimating him. As a comparison, I dated a woman in my twenties who was similar to Alfred in her abilities. She was dyslexic, with ADHD, and suffered from anxiety. She, too, was supersmart and not the kind of person whose intelligence is captured by exam testing. The difference was that she was a White girl who had grown up in an affluent area and her learning difficulties had been identified in her school. Instead of being put into remedial classes as Alfred was for the same afflictions, she was put into honors classes, given unlimited access to private tutoring, and given extra time to take important tests. When deemed necessary, she was prescribed medicines and therapy, and she went on to get a college-level education. She did not have a perfect life, because no one does, but she sure as hell had an advantage over Alfred that she herself would admit to.

Many of us have had experiences where we have been shamed for being who we are. Sometimes it can be at a covert level, where we don't always notice that it's happening. Sometimes it is obvious, and we are punished for being who we are. Those of us in the LGBTQ+ community can attest to that, too, especially those who have had to hide who they are for their own protection. Women are constantly shamed by society for the most nonsensical things: trying too hard, not trying hard enough, being too emotional, not showing enough emotion, wanting children, not wanting children—the list goes on. Let me give you an example of the minefield intersectional investors (in this case, Black women) have to navigate behind closed doors. There is a prolific Black male angel investor who by all accounts is a good person. He told me directly that part of his diligence is looking at the Instagram accounts of female founders he's considering for investment to see how they're "handling themselves in public." Not male founders, mind you, because they don't "have the same public scrutiny." Female founders. His deal flow is mostly Black female founders. He's well liked and respected and is a studious, disciplined investor with an impressive and enviable portfolio. I think he's overall a good person, but that part doesn't sit well with me, and since I'm a terrible actor and couldn't toe the party line, I missed out on an investment from him. This type of thing happens a lot, mostly with White men and women who hold the purse strings. Maintaining your authenticity under this kind of pressure, not internalizing negative messages and shrinking yourself to fit inside other people's expectations, can be really difficult. But it is so, so worth it, and the impact can be huge. I can't tell you how many times I've spoken to someone at an event who had tears in her eyes, who was shaking just talking to me, telling me about the difference seeing me be me in public has made in her life.

When I started *Your Daily Lesbian Moment!,* I wasn't just building a readership for my thoughts; I was building a community. I had feedback from readers that made me realize how important just being myself and speaking my truth could be. I would get messages from people saying that my blog had helped them understand themselves or that it had helped them to come out to their parents, or even that they had been considering suicide but reading my blog and seeing that there was a community out there and they weren't alone had changed their mind. We have the power to save lives, just by being authentically ourselves; just by being true to ourselves and not letting other people make us smaller or quieter. Is there anything more powerful than that?

16

Don't Deny the World Your Voice

Y ou—yes, you—have something to say. You are intelligent, you are unique, you are interesting, you are intriguing. You may be a visionary. Is there something that you know, something that you believe, something that you have seen or done that others could benefit from? Are there people out there who are looking for your information? There could be, and they'll never find you if you don't share what you know with the world.

At the top of 2017, back when I had massive stage fright and couldn't speak in front of fifteen or more people at a time, I remember being at a private pitch day. During the Q and A for each company, my heart raced and pounded if I even thought about asking a question. I had resigned myself to being silent, just as I had always been in such circumstances. But then I noticed something: company after company, investor after investor asked a question I had thought of. I also noticed something perhaps even more important: many questions that I had were *not* being asked by the other investors.

Nine times out of ten, they were being asked by men and by zero people of color, because I was only one of two investors of color in the room. In that moment, I felt that as scary as it was, if I didn't speak up, our voice would not be represented at all. So, with my heart pounding so loudly that I could hear my ears ringing, I raised my hand and asked my question. Once I realized that I hadn't sounded "dumb," I was still breathing, and I now had the answer to my question, I asked another a few minutes later. By the time I got to my third question, I was asking things that were outside of the box, nuanced, and weighty. I realized that I was asking questions that some people in the room might not have thought of or felt were appropriate to ask. After the pitching was over, a woman co-founder of one of the companies pulled me to the side and thanked me for asking her my question. She said no one else had asked her that in *any* investor meetings so far, and her answer was one of the things she was most proud of in general.

I've had stage fright for most of my life. I remember being in junior high and having speech class (Why oh why did I sign up for speech class?), and I never once gave a speech because every single time I was supposed to, I was "sick" that day because I was so nervous. I remember hiding behind a tree in my late twenties, when I was supposed to co-host Colorado Springs LGBT Pride. I'd had every intention of going onto that stage and co-hosting the event, but once the day came, I was like "Holy crap, how did I get here? I can't do that. I'm so nervous, I may die," and I hid behind a tree. Think about what a tree looks like. A tree doesn't have a hidden spot to it. You just walk around the other side of the tree, and you can see me. But I wasn't thinking clearly because I was so terrified. So there I was, trembling "behind" a tree while someone called my name on a microphone to introduce me. It was like that scene—spoiler alert—in the *The Sound of Music* where they're like "The family von Trapp . . ."

I started getting offers to speak at conferences and events for venture and tech after a feature story on me came out in *Inc.* in late summer 2016. I turned all of them down, of course, because I did not think it would be possible for me to get over my fear, especially within an industry where I already stood out. My biggest fear about public speaking was that I would make a fool of myself or say something stupid because of the pressure to deliver.

But as time went on, I realized I was holding back something that could be helping other people: founders, investors, and other women, people of color, and LGBTQ folks who weren't seeing themselves represented on stages at those kinds of events. I was asked to speak at the *Forbes* Under 30 Summit in October 2016, but my nerves were so overwhelming that I had to cancel. I'd already let the people there know that that was a possibility when they had approached me about the event, but I still felt disappointed in myself to have to let them down. In January 2017, I decided I would agree to do three speaking events that year. I reasoned with myself that I would do three, and if I hated doing them, if they were terrible, or I was awful at it, I'd never have to do it again.

The first thing I did to prepare for the events was to cut out the noise of everyone giving me their opinions of when and how I should "get over my fear" and instead follow my inner compass. I'd had people telling me that I had to start speaking at events because people needed to hear what I had to say, but that felt like a lot of expectations, and I knew that if I was going to do it, I would have to do it for me, on my terms.

I'd been advised by many people to try beta-blockers for my anxiety. I was unsure about that because my family has a history of heart issues, and I'd had some heart problems myself. I was scared of taking something that would slow down my heart rate. Still, I also couldn't handle the feeling of my heart beating out of my chest throughout a speaking event, so I went to talk it over with my doctor. He prescribed me a small dose and said, "Hey, just go home and try it out and have somebody with you. It's actually not that big of a deal if you use it sparingly." If your heart rate is slower, then your hands don't shake and your voice doesn't shake. Doesn't it suck when you're trying to say something and you know what you're talking about, but your voice shakes because you're having a physical reaction because your adrenaline is rushing? I took the beta-blockers for probably four months, sparingly on days I had speaking engagements. At the beginning, they were helpful, but what I noticed over time was that they didn't make a big difference. Beta-blockers aren't magic pills that make you compelling or talented, but they do take away the physical component of the racing heart, which is one less thing to worry about.

Another helpful tip for anyone with stage fright is to begin with a friendly interviewer. My first speaking event was a fireside chat with one of my good friends and someone I've invested in, Aniyia Williams, and it was in a friendly setting, a Black & Brown Founders event, talking about a friendly subject, Backstage Capital. There were about fifty people in the room, and I was so nervous. But I tell you what: as soon as I looked out into the audience, I saw a group of Black women looking back at me and smiling. I realized, "Wow, this isn't about me. This is about them. This is about the experience that they came here for, the information, the inspiration. It's not about how I feel." That moment changed everything for me, because I understood what my role was. It was no longer ego, fear, and insecurity; it was gifting.

I also found that it was useful for me or the interviewer to tell the audience that I was nervous. I was nervous for a while; it wasn't as though the nervousness went away after the first event, but I found that being honest with the audience cut out all of the tension that you build up for yourself. Simply saying "You know what, I just want to start off by saying I'm really nervous. I don't do a lot of public speaking. So just bear with me." Audiences tend to be forgiving, and most of the time they want you to win. They're not hoping that you will mess up.

I stick to what I know, and I go with the fireside chat option whenever possible, since chatting with someone is where I feel most comfortable. If I have an option, I go for the fireside every time. I also love Q and A because it keeps me on my toes. I love hearing from an audience and understanding what they really want to know and hear from me. I'm working on getting more comfortable with direct keynote TED Talk–style conversations.

I try to remember that quality matters more than quantity. Success is reaching one person on a deep level on a given day. Anything more is a bonus. I scan the audience when I first get there and I look into people's eyes, looking for someone about whom I can say, "Okay, I think I'm being helpful to them. I think this is worth it to them." If I can find that one, if I can visualize that one, that's all that matters. So it's quality over quantity. I'm not trying to get the entire room to fall in love with me. I'm trying to connect with one person, even if I never talked to that person, even if they leave and we never talk. Just the idea that one person walks away with something that helps them in some way, that is enough to fuel me for twenty, thirty, forty-five minutes.

When the nervousness starts to feel overwhelming, I repurpose it as energy that I can control and aim at will. I have a conversation with myself internally: "Okay, what is it that's wrong here? What are you really afraid of? Can you conquer that before you go out on the stage? Can you get yourself together? Have you made it more about you than it is? Do you know your topic? Is it because you don't know enough about what you're stepping into? Can you talk to someone right before you go on and maybe get a stronger feeling about what we're going to talk about? Is there something external that has nothing to do with this? Is it that you're just not having a good day?" I have that conversation with myself, and nine times out of ten, what I do is take that fear, wrap it up in some sort of protective bubble, and say, "Uh-uh, nope. All that energy inside that bubble is now energy that is going to go directly into making this as great an experience for one person in the audience as possible." That's the conversation I have with myself. I'm like "Nope, you're not going to do it today. You're not going to bring yourself down today. There are too many people trying to get in your way. You can't be one more of them."

I can guarantee you that 90 percent of what has happened in the last two years or so wouldn't have happened at the scale, the speed, the quality, or the intensity or had the impact that it has were it not for my starting to speak publicly. I never would have believed anyone who had told me that, even though they said literally those words: "Things will change for you if you do." It was one of the hardest things I've ever had to do, because I was breaking out of thirty-six years of habits.

I think I've spoken at more than 150 firesides, Q and As, pitch competitions, and keynotes since then, and each time it's been about being a voice that may not be heard otherwise. I'm no longer nervous, and thinking about the impact I could have helps me fight any residual misgivings and repurpose it as energy. I never in a million years would have thought that I would be speaking to so many people so often and be so happy to do so.

If you can be in control of your message, that's the best situation to be in. However, it's important to remember that you can't always control the narrative around your ideas. This can be a paralyzing realization; there have been many times when I have worried about being misunderstood or even misrepresented. It makes you wonder whether it's worth speaking publicly, if there is the chance that your message will be twisted.

Sharing your voice is a gift, one that you're giving to other people. I'm inspired every time I hear an underestimated person stand up and speak out. This is your time; we're in the era of podcasts, of self-publishing, of blogs and social media. You can tweet or use your Instagram account for more intentional and purposeful content. There are so many ways to communicate now. You may be asking, how can I share something if I'm not yet an expert? Share the learning process. It's so inspiring to see someone learn and to hear about the hiccups and traps on the way to becoming an expert. Remember, it's about being informative, relatable, inspirational. If your content is one or more of these three things, it's a winner. Sharing yourself, your point of view, and your gifts and talents with the world is invaluable. Only you can create content from your point of view. That's your gift to the world.

17

Rolling with the Punches

n 2017, I was given the opportunity to be the subject of a podcast called *StartUp* by Gimlet Media. Gimlet Media is a podcast platform that is well known for the diversity of its subject matter and the quality of its podcasts. It began as a start-up itself, and the first season of *StartUp* chronicled the journey of Gimlet Media founders Alex Blumberg and Matt Lieber as they pitched to investors, raised capital, and hired employees. The podcast gave listeners an inside view of the process, which I thought was really cool, so I was excited when they approached me. They were planning season seven and wanted to delve into the world of venture capitalists.

Between October 2017 and April 2018, we worked on the podcast. The host, Amy Standen, followed me around some of the time; sometimes we spoke on the phone, other times I would record my thoughts and send them to her, and occasionally I would go into the Gimlet Media office in Brooklyn and be interviewed. It was a documentary show, but sometimes it felt as though I were on reality TV, with a person holding a mic following me around and asking me to react to everything. It involved seven months of recording, so there were a lot of ups and downs within that time. I remember that when we first started recording, Amy asked me if I thought anything of note would happen for the company in the next six months. I was like "Amy, hold on to your hat!" Just by our existing, something is always happening.

Aside from following me on my journey, they also interviewed people from my life, both personal and business. I was excited when our founders were interviewed; it was a great chance to show them off to the world and to widen their audience. Gimlet Media showed me a list of people they would be interviewing or contacting for the show, and I kid you not, there were more than a hundred names on that list. There were people I hadn't seen in five or ten years, people I used to live with, people I'd been friends with for a long time—all kinds of people. I couldn't believe they would spend so much time on that. There must be hundreds of hours of taped interviews that never made it into the podcast, and I would love to hear them. Who isn't curious to know what their friends, family, and acquaintances have to say about them?

I heard the podcast at the same time as everyone else did; there was no special treatment or preview for me. This was after all a journalistic endeavor. I was anxious about how it would turn out, how they would frame it, and what some of the people on that list of names might say about me. It wasn't that I thought they would say negative things about me; I just wanted to ensure that the context was there so that their opinions weren't aired in a vacuum. As with all documentaries, the final result is all in the editing. Six hours of recording could turn into six minutes of tape.

Backstage Capital has a podcast called *The Bootstrapped*

VC, and we used it to record responses to each Gimlet episode. Each week I would listen to the episode as soon as I could, sometimes getting up very early, depending on what time zone I was in. I would first listen to the episode just as me, feeling whatever I felt, reacting in whatever way felt natural to me. Then, a few hours later, I would listen again, but this time I would try to put myself into the shoes of someone who wasn't me, who maybe didn't know me, and who was being introduced to me through the show. After that, we (me; Christie Pitts, my partner in Backstage; and Bryan Landers, Backstage's COO and producer/co-host of *The Bootstrapped VC*) would record the response episode.

I was very suspicious of Amy at first, and in the beginning I definitely tried to control how the team produced things, but that was mostly due to my history as a production coordinator; I have ideas, and I want to share them! I thought the first two episodes were great. They were accessible for people who didn't know a lot about venture capital; they spoke to members of our portfolio, which made me really proud; and I was touched by the way my personal story was laid out, particularly around my homelessness, in a way that allowed the facts to be stated but my dignity to remain intact. It was important to me that that be handled in the right way, because it isn't just my story, it's a reality for many people, and I wanted those people to feel validated; judging by the intense reaction of those who reached out to me, it definitely hit a nerve.

As the episodes continued to air, I began to feel less comfortable with some of the narrative. Throughout the series, the theme of "They're running out of money, what will they do?" was really hyped up. If you didn't know much about venture capital, it really seemed as though I was spending money willy-nilly and that my fund was about to take a nosedive. If you did know about venture capital, you knew that what Amy was talking about was standard. Amy and the producers were learning about venture capital as they made the series, and that was great for the listeners because it made the series easy to digest, but it wasn't always very accurate. I felt I was being presented as a somewhat thoughtless risk taker, but the risks I was taking were the core part of my job; venture capital is the business of risk taking. In fact, I was named one of CNN Business's "Risk Takers 2019." The majority of well-known men in venture capital are known to be risk takers, I didn't know why it should be different when I was doing it.

I felt there was a bias in the way we as a company and I as a Black woman were being presented. The producers asked me questions about the way I spend money that they wouldn't have asked a straight White man. At one point, when I met my employees Chacho Valadez and Dianne Cherrez at the airport, it was stated on the podcast that I "roll deep." It was framed as though I went everywhere with an entourage, but they weren't an entourage, they were my colleagues, members of Backstage Capital, each of whom does the work of way more than one person. There are men in venture capital who have spent their LPs' money on taking founders and team members to strip clubs and drinking in the middle of the day, yet I was being called out for taking members of my team with me to important meetings. I also believe that Amy had her own bias based on her own limitations, on what she would do in a given situation. It was counterintuitive to her to add people to the Backstage team when we were running out of runway. But as a venture capitalist, I have to play for what I know Backstage will become. I have to look into the future; if I spend all day looking at my feet, we won't get anywhere. Backstage proves what can be done by underestimated people with small resources, but just because our resources are small, it doesn't mean we should have to act small all of the time.

I should note that at that point in my career, I was also on the road almost all of the time. In 2018, I spent three hundred days traveling, so I was spending my own money on nice hotel rooms because they were not only my room but my office for the day. I was spending my own money to ensure that my travel was as easy as possible, because I was often working while flying. This is not out of the ordinary; it's just me understanding what my time is worth and investing in that.

We also clashed because of the expectation the producers had regarding my emotions. I felt as though they were trying to dramatize moments by asking me how I felt or asking me to respond in a particular way, as if my natural response was not good enough. Again, I couldn't imagine them prodding and poking a man like that, expecting tears or an emotional outpouring in response to questions or events. It was as if my being professional made me some kind of alien. There are ups and downs all the time in venture capital, as we've discussed in this book, but at no point would I place all my eggs in one basket and have everything riding on one yes. If I get a no, it sucks, but I move on. You have to roll with the punches and try not to take them personally.

At one point in the season, I received a phone call from my mother in which she told me she had been diagnosed with cancer. In the episode, Amy stated, "After a few long seconds, Arlan toggled back to business deal mode; she couldn't afford to linger on the news just yet." What actually happened was this: I steeled myself and continued the conversation in the car until we reached our destination. As soon as we arrived, I spoke to Chacho about my mother, and later on—when I was ready—I spoke to Amy about it. It was not a moment I was looking to share on tape immediately, as I needed to process it myself internally first and talk to my friends and family about it. To imply that my business was in such disarray that I couldn't "afford" to take time to think about my mother's health was insulting to Backstage, but to imply that I would ever put business or money ahead of family was more than insulting to me as a person. I didn't want my mother's health to be used as a storyline without her permission, and I was not ready to share over a microphone the devastating news that I was still processing.

In the seventh episode, we recorded live from Gimlet Fest. Amy and I were interviewed by Shereen Marisol Meraji, the host of *Code Switch*, a podcast about race and identity. It gave us the opportunity to both talk about the series and hash out any issues, and I definitely didn't mince my words when it came to talking about the bias I felt the Gimlet Media team had. They were a diverse team, so I didn't feel I was being judged by a jury whose members weren't my peers. And it wasn't the kind of bias where you're angry because you know they'll never change. It was just a bias that came from ignorance that needed to be pointed out, the kind of thing where someone doesn't realize the way they are coming across. I think Amy, the writers, and the producers were ready to take that criticism and rethink some of what they were doing, which is really positive. Amy is a great reporter, and she and the producers created a great series of podcasts.

Overall, the experience was interesting, and in retrospect, I'm happy I did it. At the time, I felt very raw from it, because it was such an intense experience and it was so personal. I would have liked the producers to have done a little more research about venture capital as an industry, as I think their lack of knowledge caused some of the misframing of events.

It was my name and my reputation on the line; when the research was wrong, I was worried about what the repercussions could be, and I took a lot of it to heart. But there are so many people who were introduced to me and to Backstage through the podcast, and so many people have messaged me to tell me how much the series inspired them. If it helped bring more people into our orbit and helped more underestimated people consider themselves future founders, venture capitalists, or angel investors, I can't be mad about that. The quality of the series—especially those first two episodes—are still some of the most elegantly produced podcasts I've ever heard, and I'm proud to have shared the stage with Backstage portfolio founders Sheena Allen, Melissa Hanna, and Brian Brackeen.

18

Ditch the Costume

Be yourself so that the
people looking for you can find you.

Social media can make you feel as though the world is providing you with everything you need to feel bad about yourself, your life, your career; you can always find someone online who is doing better than you, who is happier than you, who is busier than you. Many people will tell you how important it is to have an online presence in today's world. There are very few people who don't use some kind of social media, whether LinkedIn, Twitter, Facebook, or Instagram. Increasingly, we're using these platforms for business as well as for keeping in touch with faraway friends and Aunt Rebecca's second cousin, and we're not just using them for that purpose. I've actually found Twitter to be the most effective when it comes to finding employees; most of the first Backstage Capital employees were introduced to me via Twitter. As the founder of Backstage Capital, I use social media not only to recruit, connect with founders, and meet investors but also to highlight my work.

When you're active on social media, you share a piece of yourself with others. Sometimes this is part of a bigger strategy. You may want to be seen by a potential employer, or you may be hoping that someone will purchase something from you or learn from you. Sharing your life online can be rewarding. It can bring you new friends, it can inspire other people, and it can help you share your truth with the world. But it's important, when you do this, to be intentional. When I made the decision years ago, back when I started the *Your Daily Lesbian Moment!* blog, to share my life with an audience— whether it was five people, five thousand people, or five hundred thousand—I intentionally decided to share the good *and* the bad.

Social media is full of people sharing the good parts of their life; many people use Instagram as their personal scrapbook of achievements, and that's great, I'm not knocking it at all. But it can lead to a false perception of how well everyone else is doing. Sometimes you look through your feed and assume, based on what people are putting out into the world, that everything is going really well for them. They seem to be having hit after hit. They're blessed with constant good luck, racking up one success after another, surrounded by admiring friends and family. It's a natural instinct to put your best foot forward, posting only when things are going well. There are lots of reasons for this: maybe you don't want to impose on other people, or you don't want to bring them down. Maybe you're embarrassed by your negative emotions, or you've been taught that if you don't have anything nice to say (even about yourself), you shouldn't say anything at all. Maybe you feel as though you're failing or losing, and you're ashamed. Maybe you assume that the only thing people care about is the good stuff. Or you feel that the bad stuff is boring and doesn't make for good content. Those feelings of inadequacy and self-doubt could be imposter syndrome, which I think about all the time.

EVERYONE IS GOING THROUGH SOMETHING, NO MATTER HOW PRIVILEGED THEY ARE.

Over the past twenty years, I've met thousands of people in the real world. I've not only met them, I've sat and had deep conversations with them, people of all kinds of backgrounds, in all stages of wealth and success, from students and aspiring entrepreneurs to celebrities, musicians, and heads of companies. So I can tell you that despite how it may appear on Instagram, there is no one who is just floating. Everyone is going through something, no matter how privileged they are.

So from the very beginning, I made the decision that I would not put up a facade online. I wanted to be real. There have been many downs in my life. I don't share every single one with every single person—I do have boundaries—but I know that the time I spend online sharing my story with people should be accurately split among the good parts, the bad parts, and the parts that fall into the middle. We spend most of our lives in the middle area. To be true to ourselves, we need to share it.

I think if you share your full self with people, you are able to relate to them on a much deeper level. You may reach someone in a way that you'd never expect. Sometimes I put out a tweet, a thread of tweets, or an Instagram post in which I will describe something I have observed or explain something I believe. Over time, I'll receive countless private messages from people saying, "I really relate to what you just wrote online. I can really understand it. I can't say it myself right now because I have this job and I would get fired, but I really believe in what you're saying and it's helped me. Thank you for saying it."

Often I'm surprised by the reaction I get just from being honest. People need someone else to say what they've been thinking. Sometimes they need to see their truth reflected back to them.

YOU CAN'T CONTROL WHAT OTHER PEOPLE THINK OF YOU. YOU CAN ONLY BE AUTHENTIC EACH AND EVERY TIME.

It took me until my late thirties to understand that I can't make someone like me. I can't dictate how someone views me or what that person views as fact versus fiction when it comes to my life. It's not something that's easily learned or accepted overnight. Looking at other people to determine how I should feel about myself is a game that I am not interested in playing. It is wasted energy. You can't control what other people think of you. You can only be authentic each and every time. I have always felt a little bit like the odd person out in any given room. Sometimes it's because of my race, my gender, or my sexual orientation. Other times it's because of my thoughts on philosophy, religion, and spirituality. Or sometimes it's because I have an odd sense of humor or because I have a "strange" way of viewing things. But through good times and bad, food stamps and five-star hotels, I've always been myself.

Early on in raising my first fund, I went to New York to meet with a Black female investor. I thought that she could potentially invest in the fund, so I was very excited to meet her. She was highly regarded and very successful. About five minutes into our conversation, she told me that she didn't like the way I dressed and that I wouldn't get very far if I didn't dress up more. She said it with the best intentions; I knew she was trying to help me, but I felt an instant discomfort. I thought, "Wow, of all things to point out, of all things to be thinking about, of all my accomplishments and potential, the way I'm dressed *has* to be the least important."

Still, her comment was in my head as I walked through New York. I thought, "Should I change the way I dress? Should I dress more corporate? Or more normal? Or more 'girly'?" It took only a few minutes for me to decide, no way. I'm going to dress the way I feel comfortable, because if I don't feel comfortable, what I have to say will not come across as authentic and sincere. And if I don't come across as authentic and sincere and present my case with my vision and intelligence as the main event, I will probably lose. And so I thought, "Okay, I'm going to be myself. I'm not going to change the way I dress, because that's who I am."

I think it was less than two weeks after that New York trip that Marc Andreessen invested in our fund. Andreessen invented the web browser, for all intents and purposes, and he didn't care how I was dressed: in jeans and a T-shirt, a hoodie, and purple sneakers (for branding and for comfort). He cared about what I had accomplished so far, the potential I had, and the message I was spreading. If I had changed, if I had put on some sort of costume in order to appease others, I might have missed him, and he might have missed me! If I'd been busy worrying about how I looked and how I was appearing to people, maybe I wouldn't have spent the time talking to him online, wouldn't have written the nerdy blog post that attracted his attention to begin with, wouldn't have followed through in a timely manner to secure that bag.

SOMEONE RIGHT NOW IS LOOKING FOR YOU.

Someone right now is looking for you; someone is looking for a person who reminds them of herself and makes her feel comfortable. Right now, you as you are, your authentic self, you are that person. And if you put on a costume, she's going to walk right by you.

AND IF YOU PUT ON A COSTUME, SHE'S GOING TO WALK RIGHT BY YOU.

PART V

CREATIVITY

19

Natural Ingenuity

Black women are some of the best hackers this country has.
We know how to figure things out.

When I first learned about start-ups, founders, and the crazy world around them, it felt as though I had finally found my home. I'd worked for a paycheck since I was fifteen; I'd needed to help with the bills at home, and when I'd finished school, it hadn't felt as if college was an option for me. So I had taken jobs that helped me pay my way in the world. But I also always had other projects. There was always something I was interested in getting off the ground, something that caught my attention, whether it was a huge moon-shot idea that I knew would take years to put into action or a creative hack that I used to help me get by.

When I was in third grade, my mom took me to Sam's Club, a wholesale retailer. I can't remember what she was buying, but I'm going to assume it was probably five hundred rolls of toilet paper. Bored, I wandered down the candy aisle, amazed at the masses of brightly colored confectionery. I'd never seen candy in bulk before, and I began to imagine the possibilities. Somehow it occurred to eight-year-old me that I could sell the candy to my classmates for less than they could buy it at 7-Eleven. I had family in Jackson, Mississippi, and the best part of any trip there was always going to see the "Candy Lady" who lived down the road from my relatives. It hit me that if I bought the candy, I could be the Candy Lady! The Candy Lady of third grade! I convinced my mom to buy me a tub of Fireball jawbreakers. I took them home, set aside five for myself, and then went to 7-Eleven to check out prices and do the math. I knew I could undercut 7-Eleven and still make a profit because the Fireballs from Sam's Club had cost only pennies each. For a while, I made about $10 a week selling candy at school, which is a lot for a kid and was even more for a kid in 1989. I felt as though I was walking on air during that time; I loved being the Candy Lady, and I loved making money.

While building my career as the Candy Lady, I also set up a scratch-and-sniff sticker operation. It went like this: if you did well at school, the teacher gave you a sticker as a reward. I loved those stickers. I had a lot of them already, because I did well on my tests, but I was also kind of greedy and wanted more of them. So I spoke to every kid in my class and said, "Hey, if you give me one of your stickers, I'll keep it for the school year, and you can come and look at my collection anytime you want. At the end of the year, I'll pick a winner to take home the entire collection." Every single kid gave me one of their stickers. They knew they were taking a gamble; it was a totally transparent operation: they were risking losing one sticker in exchange for a chance of winning the whole collection of them. That school year, I had the biggest sticker collection of anyone, and I loved to carry it around with me. I'd be talking to someone and say, "Oh, hang on a minute, I just gotta—" and open up my collection of stickers and scratch and sniff one. At the end of the year, as promised, I raffled the collection and one of my classmates took it home.

Those sorts of ideas, those projects, seemed so normal to me at the time. When I look back now, I'm amazed at how my mind worked. In high school, when I needed to raise money to buy a computer, I walked from door to door in my neighborhood and offered to paint people's house numbers on the curb by their driveway. I'd noticed that some of the house numbers were hard to see, and if you had deliveries coming or you were directing people to your house, it could get confusing. So I decided to solve the problem. I got out my paint and my stencils, charged $8 apiece, and painted the numbers.

This kind of natural ingenuity runs in my family; my brother, Alfred, is a perfect example. Due to his troubles in school, his undiagnosed learning difficulties, and becoming a father at an early age, he never graduated. He had a basic, inexpensive home computer and used it to teach himself how to record, edit, mix, master, perform, and produce music. He produced several albums of his own, and he was also the creative director for the imaging and branding of his music. He did it all. He also went on to co-found RealLyfe Records, a record label in Dallas that still exists twenty years later. He was one of the leaders of a rap collective called the DecaBoyz in the 1990s and early 2000s. He sold his CDs in places such as Deep Ellum, an artsy neighborhood in Dallas, and he moved thousands of copies.

People in Silicon Valley are always talking about health

hacks, sleep hacks, productivity hacks, hacks that make life easier for other people and the founder rich. Those kinds of hacks don't feel like hacking to me; they feel like privilege. There are Silicon Valley hackers; then there are Backstage Capital hackers. The people I work with and the people I'm trying to get more opportunities for are the ones who are really hacking. When you don't have much to begin with or you're starting from less than nothing, hacking is just part of your everyday life.

I think that women with babies are the ultimate hackers. If I take a meeting with a woman and she's talking me through her business plan while feeding her baby, I'm floored by her multitasking and her ability to get things done. I don't need to ask her if she can handle starting a business while being a mother, because I've already seen that she can. If I meet someone who has never been to college, who doesn't have traditional business experience, but who has worked her way up through a retail store and has a great idea, I'm going to take that person just as seriously as I would take a Stanford graduate. I pattern match for grit, determination, and tenacity, and they can come in a whole range of different guises.

REAL INGENUITY
TAKES HARD WORK.

If you have a hack that saves you valuable time, great! If your hack is about avoiding hard work, we aren't going to see eye to eye. Real ingenuity takes hard work. The things that have traditionally turned other investors off are often selling points to me.

20

Write Your Own Invitation

I refuse to believe that there's any room
any of us don't deserve to be in.

There have been many times in my life when I could
have just given up on something because it wasn't
easy or because it wasn't clear how I could make it
happen. Difficult situations often look like impossible
situations until you see the little chink in the armor, the back
route, the work-around. Over the years, I've realized that
there is almost always a work-around. This, as you can see, is
a theme in my life. I found a way to become the tour manager
for the band goldenboy because I was bored at work and I
wasn't creatively engaged by what I was doing. I heard a song
I liked, I wanted to see it performed live, and instead of giving up when I realized that the band had no upcoming US
tour dates, I taught myself what I needed to know to make a

tour happen and created the opportunity for myself. Then I used the skills I had learned from the goldenboy tour to get jobs with other indie artists, which would later lead me into a successful career in the live music industry.

THERE IS ALMOST
ALWAYS A
WORK-AROUND.

Let me give you another more recent example. When I was first trying to get investments for my fund, I was emailing back and forth with Chris Sacca, a very successful fund manager. I met him early on through one of his limited partners (LPs) who happened to own a music venue I had worked in for a day and who was kind enough to introduce me. At that point in my journey to becoming a venture capitalist, there weren't many people who were replying to my emails, so I was very grateful to Chris for responding to my email as graciously as he did—and for any advice he could give me.

Fast forward to 2016. I was visiting San Francisco, and I went to an event where Chris was the keynote speaker. It was a big event, not the kind where you could just walk up to the person onstage. But I was determined to get some time with him and speak to him face-to-face. It's important to note that I was the only Black woman attending the event. I knew I needed to speak to him, to let him know that Black women weren't getting into these rooms and weren't getting these opportunities. I knew that if I could talk to him for just a few minutes, I could convince him to make a bet on me. Unfortunately, everyone else in the room wanted to speak to him, too, and it seemed unlikely that I would get a chance if I just waited around after the event. If I was to seize the opportunity, I would have to get creative.

As he began his keynote, I scoped out the room. I was listening to him but also looking for my opportunity. I noticed that most of the waitstaff were Black, so I went over to one Black woman who was working, who seemed as though she didn't know who Chris Sacca was and couldn't care less, and I said, "See that guy up there? I need to talk to him." She didn't ask me any questions, she just said, "Okay. He's supposed to be doing a video interview upstairs right after this. He's going to go through a back door to get upstairs. If you take this elevator, it'll take you directly to where he's going to be." Then she stood in front of the elevator, casually reached her hand back and pushed the button, and I slowly walked backward into the elevator. She gave me the eye and signaled, "One up." I pushed the button, and off I went.

When Chris arrived, I watched him sit down in the makeup chair. As soon as I saw the makeup artist drape a cloth over his shoulders, I stepped into the room, knowing he'd be there for twenty minutes, getting makeup done for the video interview. He saw me and said, "Arlan?" and I was like "Yeah, it's me, Arlan!" I proceeded to talk with him the whole time he got his makeup done. I told him about the traction I was getting for my fund and the few investors I had, and he kept asking questions. Eventually it was time for his interview, so I left the room, but I waited just outside. At one point, a founder arrived and asked me, "Is Chris Sacca back there?" and I answered innocently, "Oh, I don't know." Maybe I should have felt bad for derailing him, but I had to have my moment. Plus

I figured that founder would get another chance if he was as persistent as I was.

After the interview, Chris left the room, and there I was, waiting for him. I walked alongside him, walking and talking like they do on TV, and we picked up our conversation where we had left off. He asked, "Arlan, why don't you just get a job at a fund? Why do you have to start your own fund?" I looked at him and said, "Chris, *you* did it." "Oh," he replied. "Email me tomorrow." The next day I emailed him a follow-up, and that began the conversation that led to both him and his wife investing in my fund.

Talking my way backstage—whether at a conference, a concert, or any other kind of event I didn't have an invitation for—is something I've been doing for a long time. I'm the kind of person who, if I see a conference is happening and everyone is there with their name tag, I'm like "Oh, excuse me, my tag isn't here . . ." I once even got to the point where I was touring nationally with artists and actually had a legit backstage pass. I would sometimes take it off and see if I could get backstage—just to challenge myself and sharpen my skills.

> ## PULL YOUR OWN CHAIR UP TO THE TABLE. SCRIBBLE YOUR OWN NAME ON THE VIP LIST, AND DON'T LET ANYONE TELL YOU THAT YOU DON'T BELONG.

When you're underestimated, you're less likely to receive an invitation to the party. You don't have the same "ins" that other people have. Maybe you don't have the money or you don't have the contacts, but that doesn't mean you don't deserve to be there. Sometimes you have to write your own invitation. Pull your own chair up to the table. Scribble your own name on the VIP list, and don't let anyone tell you that you don't belong.

21

This Industry Wasn't Built for Us

Don't dim your light or change your colors for anyone.

f you're trying to break into an industry from which you've been excluded, it's important to remember that the prescribed ways of doing things won't always work for you. As a queer Black woman trying to hack my way into Silicon Valley, knowing that it was built around the lives and experiences of straight White men, I had to be innovative, and I had to trust myself. When you try to fit into a cutout that isn't your shape, you can end up contorting yourself in painful ways. I don't think we should have to contort ourselves. I don't think we should have to be uncomfortable all the time in order to fit in. I think we should grab a pair of scissors and open up the cutout so it fits a larger group of people. When you come in with the scissors, people are going to tell you, "You're crazy," "You're too much," "This just isn't the way things are done." Well, that's the point. We're not going to settle for the way things have been done in the past, because we want a future that is brighter than the present.

When something is built around one group of people's experiences, it can be unintentionally shortsighted. This is one reason I believe a diverse team creates the most useful products; it's hard to imagine problems you have never faced. Silicon Valley was built around affluent, intelligent, Ivy League–educated men. A large percentage of VCs went to Harvard or Stanford, and that's where most of their network is found.

Most investors in Silicon Valley require what is known as "a warm introduction" to new founders. What this means is that someone who knows both the investor and the founder introduces the two and basically vouches for the founder. This is a way of cutting through all of the "cold introduction" emails, wherein a founder attempts to sell an investor on her company. I can understand, knowing the amount of emails investors receive on a daily basis, the need to have some kind of vetting system in place. Unfortunately, warm introductions mean that in order to contact an investor regarding funding, you already need to know someone that person knows. Which means that you need to be already in the circle. This not only makes it difficult for those of us not in the Stanford/Harvard circle, it also makes those networks eventually stale. We may not have access to the networks that have kept straight White men in business, but we do have networks. Our personal networks and our community networks include people who are underserved, whose needs are not met by large corporations.

The homogeneity of VCs not only stunts the careers of founders, it also blocks the flow of creativity in the industry and doesn't allow for ideas that can help people outside of their particular understanding of life. Sheena Allen, the founder of CapWay (a Backstage Capital Headliner and one of our first hundred investments) has spoken about the trouble she had getting VCs to understand her company. CapWay is a financial tech start-up that aims to help the financially underserved, as well as improve financial literacy. Sheena knew from personal experience, and from talking to people in her community, that there was a significant section of American society that was not using banks. Their reasons ranged from the costs associated with having a bank account to not living near any banks to a lack of money to put into a bank account to a distrust of the banking industry. Sheena knew that this was a group of underserved people who weren't being reached by larger banking corporations, which couldn't understand their mindset. When she spoke to VCs about CapWay, however, she found that most of them were shocked by the idea that there were people in America who didn't have a bank account. They didn't feel this was an idea with growth potential, because they underestimated how many underserved people there were; it didn't tally with their personal experience and their view of the world. When I first began looking for LPs to invest in my company, I had no bank account. I understood the world Sheena was coming from. Knowing your community helps you provide innovative solutions to their problems; when you are facing people who don't understand, trust that you are the expert.

When you're privileged (and we all are in some way), it can be easy to assume that there are some things that everyone has: stable housing, access to the internet, free time to pursue ideas, a bank account. Some people may never have had to consider what it would be like not to have one of these things, let alone all of these things. When I was sleeping at the airport, in motels, in Airbnbs, I was doing all I could to ensure that the VCs I was contacting didn't know my housing situation. I knew that if they thought of me as homeless at that early point in my career, when I just wanted someone to take a chance on my company, they wouldn't have been able to think of me as a future venture capitalist. What I've proven is that you can be both: the person unsure of where she'd be sleeping that night and the person with the vision to lead an investment company.

There have been times in my career when I've had to be innovative to keep Backstage going, to ensure that my mission and vision continue. When Backstage needed more investment, I began to sell my personal investment profit percentage (known as "carry") in our Headliners. This is not something that most VCs do, and it could affect my own future wealth. But I'm not most VCs. I'd like to retire wealthy, but it's more important to me that Backstage exists and is able to invest in these overlooked companies, until it no longer needs to exist.

We built Backstage Studio as a way to create revenue to invest in Backstage Capital. I realized early on in the Backstage journey that we as a company cannot follow the same path as every other investment company, because our journey has been different from the start. We're hoping to end up at the same destination, but we don't have to take the same road. This is why it sometimes wears on me when Backstage is compared to other VC firms. We're different from everything that has existed up to this point. You cannot make direct comparisons to other VC firms and say that we are or are not successful. We're a whole new ecosystem, and we can't be boxed in. I told you, we brought the scissors.

We can't be apologetic for who we are, where we came

from, what we do and don't know, or what we think. We can't live in a role cast by others, created by others; we have to be ourselves. Maybe we don't fit in, and maybe we don't need to. I won't apologize for being enthusiastic or curious or determined. I won't let others think that there is only one way to be in this industry or in any industry. Innovation comes from having the courage to be different and to do things differently.

PART VI

CONFIDENCE

22

Imposter Syndrome

You can't compare your chapter 2
to someone's chapter 10.

Very few of us feel ready for the positions we are put into, whether through starting a new job, getting a promotion at work, starting your own company, or becoming a parent. Very few of us, especially women, feel that we're worthy of it. We talk down to ourselves, saying things that we would never say about our loved ones. We walk around feeling like frauds, second-guessing ourselves and trying to push down the fear that someone is going to find out that we don't know what we're doing. Imposter syndrome is an epidemic, and it affects underestimated people more than most.

IMPOSTER SYNDROME IS AN
EPIDEMIC, AND IT AFFECTS
UNDERESTIMATED PEOPLE
MORE THAN MOST.

The cool thing about talking to so many people over the years is that I have started to see patterns that are inherent in all of us. What I have noticed is that we all have some sort of insecurity that can be leveraged against us—but only if we let it. Minimizing that insecurity in yourself is key.

A lot of insecurity comes from making comparisons between things that aren't equal. Someone who has been working in a role for ten years is probably going to be better at it or will at least have more experience than someone who is just starting out. And that's okay! Why do we expect ourselves to be perfect immediately when there is so much growth and learning that come with time and experience? We would never compare a newborn baby with a ten-year-old child and say, "Ah, this baby just doesn't have what it takes. She can't even speak! Or walk! Or do simple multiplication! She clearly isn't going anywhere in life." When you're being hard on yourself, imagine someone saying the same thing to your best friend, your partner, or one of your parents. Then think about how ridiculous it is, and feel free to laugh with yourself!

EVERYONE IS HOPING TO BE ACCEPTED
AND TO BE APPRECIATED AND UNDERSTOOD;
IT DOESN'T MATTER IF THEY'RE BROKE
OR THEY'RE BILLIONAIRES.

At the end of the day, everyone wants the same things in life. Everyone is hoping to be accepted and to be appreciated and understood; it doesn't matter if they're broke or they're billionaires. You have to remember that you're not the only person who's ever felt this way. I spoke at a fireside chat a few months ago, and the organizer asked those in the audience, which was composed of high-powered women, to raise their hands if they'd ever felt imposter syndrome. *All of them* raised their hands. As they looked around at one another, I could see that they were shocked and pleasantly surprised to find that they were not alone.

In October 2017, I was invited to speak at Summit LA17, which was advertised as "The world's preeminent ideas festival." Having never been previously invited, all I knew of Summit LA17 was that it was invitation only, exclusive, and held on a boat. In 2017, it was moved from the high seas to a hotel in downtown Los Angeles, and I was asked to speak. I was excited about it, and because it was local, I went alone, without any of the Backstage Crew. There were a lot of well-known people there: Jeff Bezos was headlining it; Shonda Rhimes was speaking, and so were Malcolm Gladwell and Reed Hastings, the co-founder and CEO of Netflix. Tickets to the festival cost anywhere between $2,000 and $10,000, and I didn't think anybody would pay that kind of money to come see me. When I arrived, I headed to the room I would be speaking in. It was a small room that held maybe a hundred seats, and I was so excited. I was taking video for Instagram, saying, "Okay everybody, come to this room," because I wanted to get as many people as possible in there. I went and introduced myself to the sound engineer. She was really excited to meet me and said, "Oh, did they tell you? This isn't your room anymore." My immediate thought was "Oh, okay, not enough people showed interest in my talk, and there are a lot of big names here and they need the room." I was disappointed, but only because I'd already tweeted about the room and put it on Instagram. The sound engineer said she was upset because she had learned about me and had been hoping to be the person to do my sound, and I assumed she was trying to make me feel better about being downgraded.

Then she said, "Let me take you to the new room." She led me down the hall, and I was looking into all these doorways that we were passing, wondering, "How far away is this room? Is she going to take me outside and close the door behind me?" We got to the main lobby, and she turned to me and whispered, "There's something going on right now," and put her finger to her lips. Then she opened the door and whispered, "This is it."

It wasn't the door to go outside. It was the main hall, and it was absolutely huge. I was so confused, I had to ask her what we were doing there. She said, "This is your room! What did you think?" I explained that I'd thought we were going to a smaller room or maybe a closet; that I assumed I had been downgraded out of lack of interest. And she explained, "We looked at the app this morning, and there were so many people who had signed up to see you that we had to actually bump someone so that you could have this room." I couldn't believe it. When it was my turn to speak, the place was packed, and not only that, it was packed with mostly White men. It was the first time I'd seen a room of that size full of people wanting to hear what I had to say. It was at that point I thought, "Okay, this is definitely something. Something is brewing here."

Unfortunately, underestimated groups suffer from imposter syndrome partially because they are often perceived as and treated as imposters by the wider society. I've come across this myself many times over the past few years, especially when I've shown up to a speaking engagement at a conference or a meeting at a fancy hotel and been asked for my ticket, for proof that I'm meant to be there. This has happened when I've been the headlining speaker at a conference. My face is in the program. It's on the poster. And still there's the person taking tickets with a skeptical look on their face, waiting for the A-OK from someone who looks "more legit." Eventually someone hurries over, embarrassed, and vouches for me. The problem is, people don't expect to see us in certain locations or in specific roles. We're expected to be in the background, helping someone more important, bringing out the lunch or clearing away the plates. We carry this around all the time, the flicker of confusion on the face of a White man the moment he realizes that maybe he's supposed to be paying you attention, that maybe you aren't meant to be invisible. Sometimes it's the momentary surprise on a person's face when you show up to your first meeting, because, oh, they never expected you to be . . . different. All of this weighs us down and piles onto the imposter syndrome we already feel and compounds our internal self-doubt.

Not only that, but the standards for us are different. We don't just have imposter syndrome to contend with, we have what I like to call, "Impos . . . sible to Live Up to These Double-Standard-Ass Measures of Success the Institution Keeps Setting and Changing Syndrome"! When I started Backstage Capital, I was told that in order to be considered a success story, I would need to earn a tenfold return on my investments, rather than threefold like other venture capitalists. Anything lower, and I would be considered a failure. There are literally different rules for underestimated people!

I WILL NOT SHRINK MYSELF TO MAKE SOMEONE ELSE MORE COMFORTABLE. I DESERVE TO BE IN THE ROOM.

I'm here to say: We do not have time for this. We cannot be slowed down by this. We need to be extra confident, extra sure of ourselves; we need to give ourselves 1,000 percent permission to do whatever it is we want to do. Confidence isn't just a hack, it's a superpower, and it's one we need to harness. How? Well, it's different for everyone, and you need to find what works for you, but here are a few things I find helpful.

1. I listen to music. Before a big meeting, before I go onstage, anytime I'm feeling those little doubts creep in, I listen to the songs that empower me:

   "Get Up 10" by Cardi B

   "Battle Cry" by Angel Haze

   "New Agenda" by Janet Jackson

   "Skyscraper" by Demi Lovato

   "Price Tag" by Jessie J

   "Red Light" by Jonny Lang

   "Follow Your Arrow" by Kacey Musgraves

   "Roar" by Katy Perry

   "Keep Your Head Up" by 2Pac

   "CRZY" by Kehlani

   "Fly" by Rihanna and Nicki Minaj

   "All I Have" by NF

   "Try" by P!nk

"Chandelier" by Sia
"Run This Town" by Jay-Z and Rihanna
"This Moment" by Janine
"Somebody Loves You" by Betty Who

2. I "dress for success" in my own way, making my own rules. For some people, dressing for business means wearing a suit, it means power dressing, and it gives them added confidence. For me, power dressing is comfortable clothes and shoes, because for me to feel confident, I have to feel like myself. I can't feel as though I'm wearing a costume. If I wore a suit and heels every day, I would feel as though I was pretending to be someone I'm not, and that would make me second-guess myself. My go-to is dark jeans, a hoodie, and purple shoes (always purple shoes). Try it out; see what outfit makes you feel the most confident, the most like your authentic self: the self that knows your business plan or your résumé or your portfolio is solid, the self that knows you are not to be messed with.

3. Whenever I doubt myself or I worry that I might be overstepping or thinking too big, I ask myself, "What would a White male do?" That usually snaps me right out of it! If it's an idea he would pitch, if it's a question he would ask without embarrassment, if it's a move he would make, there's no reason I shouldn't do the same. As long as I believe in it.

4. I tell myself every day: I deserve to be here. I worked my ass off. I will not shrink myself to make someone else more comfortable. I deserve to be in the room.

5. I refuse to compare my chapter 2 with someone else's chapter 10. When others make unfair comparisons, I call them out, and when I find I'm starting to make comparisons, I call myself out. If you don't give yourself room to grow, learn, and make mistakes, you'll never make it to your chapter 10.

6. I take comfort in community. No matter what you're going through, no matter how much you doubt yourself or how degraded you feel by someone questioning your ability, someone else will have had that feeling. So find your community, and reach out to it. I use Twitter for this all the time. I'll tweet about the microaggressions that have bothered me that day, and I'll get a hundred replies either commiserating, telling me similar experiences other people have had, or just supporting me and reminding me that I have what it takes. We're stronger together.

Here's what I know: everyone has imposter syndrome because we're all figuring out this thing called life. Everyone you're jealous of is jealous of someone else, and there are people out there wishing they were you. So just remember: you're human, you're flawed, and everybody has to start somewhere. If you know those things, you're ahead of the game.

23

Everyone Deserves Empathy

Everyone you're jealous of is jealous of someone else, and there are people out there wishing they were you.

n the fall of 2018, I was one of the featured speakers at *Vanity Fair*'s New Establishment Summit. It was really a cool day. I was put up in a suite in a fancy Beverly Hills hotel, along with a lot of others who would be speaking at the summit. Even though the venue was just down the road at the Wallis Annenberg Center for the Performing Arts, a car service was provided for us in case we wanted to go back and forth from the venue. My mom flew in from Texas, and one of my best friends, Dianne, was able to attend, too.

I got to the venue around 11:00 A.M., and I was due to speak just shortly after that. In the hall I saw two other female venture capitalists I knew, Jessica Verrilli from Google Ventures and Kirsten Green from Forerunner Ventures. They both hugged me and wished me luck, knowing I would be onstage soon. It was really cool to see them because over the years, both of them are people I have looked up to. They are shining examples of why there should be more women writing checks. Just days before the summit, Kirsten had announced a $360 million fund that she had raised. Jessica had previously had a big role at Twitter and was now killing it at Google Ventures, so it was just great to have their support and to see them doing so well.

My mom, Dianne, and I went backstage and ended up sitting across from the current CEO of Uber and current CEO of Disney and of course, as you do, Alanis Morissette. Now, I have been listening to Alanis's music since I was thirteen or fourteen years old, so I nearly lost my mind when she walked in, but I held it together quite nicely, I think. She had an all-white suit on. She looked great. She had recently cut her hair really short, so it was a very different Alanis than we'd been used to seeing. She looked wonderful, and she was all smiles the entire time.

A few months prior to this, I had seen her perform at the Hollywood Bowl, at the tribute to Linkin Park's Chester Bennington. It was a night to remember in and of itself. I was there with my then girlfriend Anna (who is now my wife), who had been deeply inspired by Chester. He was the reason she had gotten into music as a performer and creator, and his untimely death had devastated her, so getting her tickets to this event had been my highest priority from the second I knew it was happening. It was a beautiful night—three hours of some of the best performances I've ever seen, including a couple dozen of acts who had all been friends of Chester and had come to make music in his honor.

In a night full of memorable and haunting performances,

Alanis's was my favorite. She performed a song called "Rest," which was about giving people in the public spotlight a break. She mentioned that celebrities with depression and addiction issues had been bad-mouthed a lot, and the song seemed to be a plea to the public for empathy. It touched me, and it was one of the first times she had ever performed it live. Watching her sing it, you knew it was deeply, deeply personal.

He's been hurting for a while
Can we cut this man some slack
And let him lie down, let him lie down

EVERYONE DESERVES
YOUR EMPATHY,
EVEN IF THEY SEEM
AS THOUGH
THEY DON'T NEED IT.

It wasn't just about Chester; it was a song about her own life, too, and I thought it was really clever, timely, and emotionally stirring. Sometimes we make fun of celebrities; we laugh off the idea that they can have a bad life. But if you think about it, most celebrities have struggles just like the rest of us. They have to live with the constant worry about their personal boundaries being breached, their every move being watched, and their mental health being at risk because of the attention and the pressure. Everyone deserves your empathy, even if they seem as though they don't need it. I actually have great empathy for celebrities in general.

Now, just a few months later, I was standing in a room not

more than ten feet away from Alanis Morissette. We were both speakers at the same event. Not just that; we were actually speaking on the *same stage*. It was one of the most surreal moments I'd had in the last couple of years.

I was on the cover of *Fast Company* at the time, and I was carrying copies around with me so I could hand them out to anyone I felt needed to see it. I grabbed a copy of the magazine out of my backpack, and I very casually sauntered up to Alanis. To be honest, I wasn't nervous, I was just excited. I felt as though I was supposed to be there, as though that moment was supposed to happen, and I trusted that she would receive me well. I said, "Alanis, my name is Arlan, and I'm speaking a little bit later. I love you, and I had the honor of seeing you at Chester's tribute at the Hollywood Bowl. It was really meaningful to me."

She looked me in the eyes with a look of deep understanding. It felt like we had broken down the facade of being in a greenroom around famous people; it was like a connection, a thank-you. I was hoping that I wasn't making her sad by reminding her of Chester, but she gave me one of those pensive smiles, as though she knew what we were talking about. Then I said, "It would be an honor to give you this magazine that I'm on the cover of." She looked at the cover and said, "It would be an honor to receive it."

It was almost as though she was singing to me, because that's totally something she would have said in an Alanis Morissette song. I handed the magazine to her, and she held it to her chest a little bit, and she just smiled really big. I can still see her smile—wide, almost childlike. She said, "This is great. I can't wait to read it." She put it away, and I can only imagine and hope that she did read it.

24

Don't Let Anyone Drink Your Diet Coke

n 2018, the evening of the Vanity Fair New Establishment Summit, I was invited to a special speaker's event hosted by Yuri Milner, the tech investor who purchased two homes in California, each of which is worth $100 million or more. The event was held in one of those homes and was co-hosted by Jeffrey Katzenberg, who is well known for his work at Disney and was awarded the National Medal of the Arts as the CEO of DreamWorks Animation. I spoke onstage with Lydia Polgreen, the editor in chief of *Huffington Post*. As I walked around the venue after I spoke, people came up to me left and right saying how much they had enjoyed the conversation, how honest and transparent I had been. Some people said that I was a breath of fresh air, which is a compliment I often get at events that are a bit more stuffy, such as financial events and sometimes tech events. To hear people say that at a *Vanity Fair* event, where it's very liberal and people take themselves less seriously, meant even more to me.

I took my mom as my guest. When we drove into the

grounds of the property, it looked like a resort, like the opening you would see in a movie or when entering Disneyland. That was the front yard. Upon arrival, we were handed champagne, which I handed back, explaining that I don't drink. One of the first people we met when we got inside was the CEO of a unicorn company, meaning a billion-dollar company. We had a great conversation, looking around and talking about how the house was so big that we could probably live in one of the wings for several weeks without anyone knowing.

As we walked further into the house, I saw Katie Couric; the editor in chief of *Vanity Fair*, Radhika Jones; and my friend Moj Mahdara, who is the CEO of Beautycon Media, a Backstage Capital portfolio company. Everywhere I looked, there was a different celebrity or some sort of millionaire or billionaire. When we got into the room where the dinner would be served, we saw that the seating was assigned. We found our table, where my mom and I were seated across from each other. She was seated next to the CEO of a major media company, and I was seated next to Jeffrey Katzenberg. At that point, I knew someone must be looking out for me, to put me next to the co-host and the most powerful person in the room. Not only was he powerful, but he was also someone who enjoyed a good narrative and had an incredible story himself.

I ordered a Diet Coke from one of the butlers dressed like a penguin, and he brought it to me, white towel over his arm, on a silver tray and set the cold can of Diet Coke and a glass down in front of me. Then I spotted Jeffrey coming over to take his seat. He is a smaller dude, very inward, and doesn't talk a lot. You can tell that he's always paying attention to everything and observing everything. He came over and was cordial. He said "Hi" to everyone at the table and then to me. We sat down. Then he reached for my Diet Coke.

I immediately stopped him and said, "No, no, no. That is my Diet Coke. You do not drink that. I can get you another one." He looked at me with a sort of interested surprise, with a look on his face that was more animated than I had seen in the previous five minutes. I think he was genuinely shocked that someone had said "no" to him and that someone would say "no" to him about something so petty. Maybe he thought I was joking at first, but I was dead serious, because I was very excited about that Coke. It was the right temperature! It tasted great! I hadn't had one all day! It was exactly what I wanted at that moment, and he was not going to take it away from me. Also, I don't like to share germs, and I assume that he doesn't, either.

He said, "Fine. Okay. Thank you," and I quickly found another penguin gentleman, who swiftly brought him the coldest Diet Coke you've ever seen that wasn't frozen. Then we sat there at that posh dinner table in that fancy room with golden accessories in the most expensive private building I've ever been in, and as everyone conversed about their fame and fortune over fine dining and drinks, Jeffrey Katzenberg and I discussed Diet Cokes and life.

Listen, you don't touch my Diet Coke. I don't care if you're the pope, you don't do it. I later learned that Jeffrey drinks twelve to thirteen Diet Cokes per day, and so in this $100 million home of his friend, where he was co-hosting that dinner for *Vanity Fair,* he had assumed that whereas everyone else was getting wine, champagne, or water, of course that Diet Coke was his. He had assumed that someone had anticipated his desire for a Diet Coke. He hadn't known that I

would be there, that I would be sitting next to him, and that I
also love a good Diet Coke.

PEOPLE WHO HAVE MORE MONEY THAN YOU OR MORE SUCCESS OR MORE FRIENDS ... AREN'T INHERENTLY BETTER THAN YOU.

People who have more money than you or more success or
more friends—or whatever else it is that makes you feel
intimidated—aren't inherently better than you. You are both
just humans at the end of it all, and you both deserve an equal
amount of respect. I don't know what would have happened
if I had let him have that Diet Coke, but I do know I wouldn't
have been able to look at myself in the mirror with as much
conviction as I can today. Jeffrey introduced me to many,
many people that night, and we followed up via email afterward. It just goes to show you that if you stay true to yourself,
things are most likely going to turn out all right.

25

I Came for the Cake, Not the Crumbs

The absolute most important thing I've learned in the past three years is the value of my time. It has been by far the most impactful driver for me for raising investment money, generating revenue, and earning income.

Some years ago, I started asking for what I'm worth and accepting nothing less. A funny thing happened: I started getting it. You have to be prepared for those who say no. But as long as you're willing to walk away when that happens, people who understand your true value will come along.

When I first began my journey of conquering my stage fright, I didn't have a lot of confidence in what I had to offer. For the first full year, I spoke at events for free. I would speak at firesides, and as time went on, those firesides were getting bigger and bigger, going from maybe forty or fifty people to four hundred or five hundred and more.

Around the summer of 2018, I decided that it was time for me to start being paid for those events. The information I had was valuable and the experience I had was valuable, so why wasn't I sharing in the value I was bringing to those events? I was inspiring people, I was driving attendance, yet the companies that hosted me were making all the money off the ticket sales.

Another thing that was valuable was my time—because if I was doing a speaking event, that meant time was being taken away from me, time that I could spend doing something else. That's when I realized that my time is a valuable asset. Running my company, Backstage, is the most important thing. Speaking events would have to get in line.

Even though I knew that charging a speaking fee was the right thing to do, I was nervous. I decided on a figure based on information I had about other speakers, advice I got from various people, and the amount of money I'd be missing out on by not being somewhere else doing something else. The number was big. It was much more than I had ever made to do anything for forty-five minutes, but I said to myself, "That's the number I'm going to ask for. If someone doesn't take it, that's fine. That means I shouldn't go, and I will spend that time doing something just as valuable, if not more valuable."

So the next time an offer came in, as they often do, I said, "Great, yes. My honorarium is this amount, and this is my travel stipend." The company came back and said, "Absolutely not. No way. We do not spend money on this. We have no budget for it." I had to make a decision: Should I write back and say, "That's okay. I'll do it for free. I'll do it for the exposure. I'll do it for the experience. I'll do it for the relationship." Or should I stand my ground and say, "Okay, this is what I knew could happen, but I don't work for free and I'm not going to say yes. Catch me next time." I replied, "Okay, that's fair enough. You don't have the budget for it and we're not going to accept." It was a really fun event that I was sad to miss out on, but I reminded myself that I had taken a stance, and that made missing the event totally worth it.

The next request that came in was from a company that had more money and that made a lot of money from ticket sales, and I knew that it could afford my fee. I was ready for the people there to say yes, but when I told them my rates, they came back and said, "Absolutely not, we are not able to do that." I said to myself, "Wow, okay. Maybe I'll never get paid to speak." But I didn't back down; I replied, "Okay, that's fine. I'll do something else that day."

Then a third inbound request came my way, and again I said, "Okay, this is my honorarium. This is my travel stipend." This time, the organizer said, "Oh, we actually have a budget for twice that much, so we'd like to offer you that, and we will take care of all your travel, and a plus one, of course." That day, I officially doubled my rate.

When I made it to the cover of *Fast Company* in October 2018, my rate went up again. Then again on New Year's Day 2019. Once I decided what I felt my time, insight, information, and inspiration were worth, I stuck to my guns. Once I stuck to my guns, I started getting what I asked for. If I had never asked, I would still be speaking for free (though I did make a deal with myself to do some events pro bono at my discretion).

YOU HAVE TO KNOW
WHAT VALUE YOU BRING,
PLACE A PRICE ON
YOUR TIME AND TALENT,
AND THEN ACCEPT
NOTHING LESS.

No matter how you make a living or what your skill set is, you have to know what value you bring, place a price on your time and talent, and then accept nothing less.

PART VII

SELF-CARE

26

The Danger of Hustle Porn

Self-care is about recognizing your value.

Silicon Valley has a reputation for encouraging dangerous working habits. From all-night hackathons to office buildings that provide everything employees could need so that they go home only to sleep, a dangerous precedent has been set. I'm here to tell you, you don't need to do all that to be successful. Don't sleep when you're dead! Sleep while you're alive and can enjoy it! The tough-love mantra that has pervaded tech culture isolates a lot of people; not everyone can work every hour of the day, pull all-nighters, or be "on" 24/7. It's unsustainable, and it disproportionately affects underestimated people. Let's face it, Silicon Valley has been built around the lifestyle of wealthy White men, and if we want to diversify that culture, we have to make some changes.

DON'T SLEEP WHEN
YOU'RE DEAD!
SLEEP WHILE
YOU'RE ALIVE
AND CAN ENJOY IT!

We have to stop asking people to prove themselves by giving companies an excess of their time. As an employer, I want my employees to love their jobs, but I also want them to have a life outside their jobs. I want them to be fulfilled people, I want them to go home, rest, and come back to work feeling energized. I want them to have the flexibility to work around whatever life throws at them. When we expect the same working patterns from every employee, we are excluding a proportion of people who could make excellent employees. When we ask employees to stay late or drop their weekend plans, we are telling potential employees that if they have kids or caring responsibilities, they shouldn't bother applying. When we make our employees feel as though they have to work until they drop every day and then come back and do it again, we're telling potential employees with chronic illnesses not to apply. When we enforce evening socializing and happy hours, we're telling our introverted colleagues that they're not as hardworking because they want downtime and alone time. We're cutting out a huge percentage of the workforce who could be the ones who turn the company around, who are just as intelligent, innovative, and talented. When we ask our employees to be robots, to work and work and just occasionally eat and sleep, we're preventing them from being people who can relate to the average working person. We're preventing them from being in their communities and from seeing problems that need fixing. We're preventing them from being creative, from being inspired, from being human. If we want a robot workforce, it's not as though we don't have the technology to build one. But robots don't do innovation, and that's what keeps Silicon Valley in business.

WE HAVE TO STOP ASKING PEOPLE TO PROVE THEMSELVES WITH AN EXCESS OF THEIR TIME.

This industry is also obsessed with "hustle." And I get it, hustle is great. I've grown up hustling for what I need, and when you see someone succeed through hustle, it can be really inspiring. But if we place too much emphasis on it, reality can be obscured.

Last year a woman contacted me to tell me she'd taken a one-way flight to Los Angeles, was sleeping in the airport, and wouldn't go home until she had met me and pitched me. She slept there for at least five nights. You can see how that mirrors my own story and why she thought I might see the stunt as an impressive display of determination, hustle, and grit. But I didn't. I felt that she was glorifying one of the hardest times of my life, something I had done out of necessity, not to get attention. It felt like a stunt, and I didn't appreciate her pushing my personal boundaries by refusing to take no for an answer. Part of the reason I started Backstage Capital was to create opportunities such as our accelerator program, so that no one has to sleep at the airport. I don't want people to have to go through what I did. When we glamorize hustle, we encourage this kind of behavior.

SELF-CARE DOESN'T
HAVE TO BE
INSTAGRAMMABLE.

I want us to trade in hustle for self-care. That's the hack I want to advocate for: sleeping, resting, taking a moment of quiet. Turning off. Over the past few years, self-care has become a buzzword, embraced by the Instagram community and the endless photos of bubble baths, spas, champagne, shopping sprees—things that can feel very much out of reach. Self-care has become an industry worth billions of dollars. But true self-care, despite what all the marketing would have you believe, doesn't have to cost money. It's all in the name: *self*-care. Caring for yourself, showing yourself some care. This can be whatever works for you: cooking yourself a meal instead of ordering takeout, or ordering takeout instead of having to cook. It depends on your life and your circumstances. Self-care doesn't have to be Instagrammable. It can be just a moment sitting down with your eyes closed. Or a twenty-minute walk. Getting your house chores done. Prioritizing these things will absolutely help your productivity overall.

My approach when facing big decisions in business or working on major strategy for Backstage and beyond is the same as my approach to dealing with personal decisions. It's the same formula I used five years ago, when I was broke: I read, I rest my body and my mind, I reflect and regroup; then I repeat. When you have huge choices to make, whether about investing someone else's money, whether you should leave your job, or whether you can afford your apartment, the most important thing to do is *pause*. Take a deep breath. Assess the situation, your surroundings, and your circumstances, and reflect. When it feels as though everything is on top of you and you have no time to do anything but think about this problem and how you will solve it, this is the moment to stop and take that time. You will always waste more time if you don't use it strategically, and taking a break to think and reflect is always a strategic use of time. I try to do this as often as I can and at least once a week.

Resting is important in so many ways. If you think about people who go to the gym, the ones who get the best results, if they're in it to chisel their bodies and build muscle, are not the ones who go in seven days a week; it's the ones who go in every other day and let their muscles and their bodies rest in between. The same applies to our minds and our mental bandwidth. Going full on seven days a week with no rest, "grinding," "hustling," whatever you want to call it, all of that to me is problematic and dangerous thinking.

SOMETIMES TIME AND SPACE ARE YOUR BIGGEST ALLIES.

Instead of working on a project nonstop, how about putting into place an absolutely mandatory day off in your schedule, a day for just thinking? I know that if you're an entrepreneur, it's really hard for you to separate your life from your job, but thinking is still work; you're still working on your company and, in fact, the rest day could be the most important day of your week, as it is in mine. You are forced to just relax, put music on, go for a walk, go for a bike ride, go for a hike, go for a drive, get on a train and watch the scenery pass you by—anything that works for you, just to think through strategy. Let your thoughts settle, let your ideas take form and shape, let time go by. Sometimes time and space are your biggest allies.

Once you've done that and you've paused and reflected, you need to regroup. You need to collect everything you have learned, pull yourself up by the bootstraps, and decide what you're going to do. What will be your next play? What will be your next move? Commit to it.

Before I started using this technique, I was a mess. I was a wreck. I put the world on my shoulders. I still carry the world on my shoulders in a way; I still worry all the time about money and operating expenses and my employees' medical insurance. I think about all that stuff, but I do it in a more measured, calm place, and we're all better off for it. The best thing I can do for the team I'm trying to lead is to be of sound body and mind.

27

Giving Up Drinking

I realize now the thing that helped me survive the later stages of my drinking addiction was that I learned to forgive myself each morning. It took years to learn that, but once I did, it was the first major step toward finally getting the help I needed to stop. One hundred–plus weeks later . . . :]

had my first taste—literally a sip—of alcohol (Alizé, to be exact) when I was a teenager. But I didn't drink a full glass until I was twenty-one. I became addicted to it sometime around the age of twenty-five and spent months at a time without a sober day. I was what is called a "high-functioning alcoholic," which meant that most people in my close circle did not realize I had a problem. It also meant that I was able to get things done in a way most people couldn't imagine that someone who was poisoning herself the way I was would be able to.

It was around the age of twenty-seven that I realized I had

a *big* problem. I was living with two British women who were in LA on a temporary visa to take acting classes, and on occasion we would have house gatherings where we invited musician friends over to perform unplugged. One day as we were getting ready for one of those intimate get-togethers, I saw a row of empty vodka bottles in the bar area that was built into our home. I asked one of my roommates who had "killed" all of the bottles of vodka. She must have thought I was kidding (or drunk, because I probably was). With a bewildered look, she said, "Arlan . . . you did."

I remember being in complete and utter disbelief, almost to the point of surrealness. It felt absurd to look at half a dozen or so empty fifths of vodka and imagine that I'd somehow (a) gone through so much alcohol so quickly, (b) had the time to do it, and, most disturbingly of all, (c) not even realized it.

Back then I was spending four or five nights per week hanging out and partying with friends in West Hollywood, with two friends in particular who would compete with each other to see who could reach for the check first. Can you believe that? An alky's dream. I was in my twenties, living in Los Angeles, writing a successful blog, and spending lots of my time with good friends who also drank heavily, so I figured that I was just doing what twentysomethings do. Besides, some of the people I knew did hard drugs and/or took pills, so I reasoned that I was the "straightest one" in the group (which was ironic for more than one reason).

The truth was, I drank more alone than I did socially. I had also convinced myself that it was okay to start drinking earlier in the day as long as I'd had lunch. This was my rule: as long as I'd had something to eat, it was okay to drink. That's how an addict's mind works, by the way, at least in my case. I think of addiction as similar to the stages of mourning one goes through when grieving a lost loved one. The eating rule was part of my bargaining stage.

To make matters worse, I'd built up a tolerance so strong that I could drink five or six Jack (Daniel's) and (Diet) Cokes or screwdrivers (vodka and orange juice) or kill a bottle of wine and still not get a severe hangover. And it didn't help that there were people in our close-knit group who had the means to fight over who would pay for rounds.

I won't go into what my rock bottom was, because it's more private than I am willing to share at this time. But it started with more than a dozen servings of hard liquor in an evening, and it happened at the end of my twenties. I was hungover for nearly three days and thought I might die. Soon afterward, I found the willpower to go sober cold turkey. I spent nearly a year and a half sober, because by that point I knew that if I didn't, I would die of an overdose or by falling down stairs while drunk or by vomiting in my sleep and inhaling the vomit, or my body would simply give out one day. That was how bad it had gotten.

Those were the hardest eighteen months. Every day I was tempted. It got easier over time, for sure, but it was rough. Prior to that dry spell, the longest I'd gone without drinking was two weeks. And anytime I reached the two-week milestone, I'd celebrate—with a drink. I was and am proud of myself for remaining sober through my thirtieth birthday celebration and through a lot of personal heartache. But as I'm sure you've guessed by now, it didn't last.

When I returned to drinking in my early thirties, it went well for a few weeks. I was drinking just enough to get myself buzzed for a few hours, so I wouldn't have to face my day or my circumstances. I even lied to myself and thought I had some power over when to stop each day. Ha! Never have I ever. The real trouble started just over a month after I started drinking again. Once again I would drink myself into oblivion to mask the pain and humiliation of being in a bad relationship or not having a place to live or not having any money or losing my business or feeling fat—whatever was going on that particular day. Because I had aged, the hangovers became more frequent and more gut wrenching. To this day, I have never felt physical pain that matches my worst hangovers.

Fast-forward to summer 2017, when I was attending WeHo Pride. I had VIP passes (which means free liquor and close proximity to the stage for concerts—but mostly free liquor) and had myself a gay old time. I remember drinking a couple of vodka diets at home (alone) to preparty (aka go numb in order to face people), then a couple more once I got to the event. Then I paid for a couple more when my drink tickets ran out. Then I called my homie Dianne, and we searched for a nightcap near last call. It was a desperate search, because ever since my second drink, I'd been in hunting mode. Some of you will recognize that feeling well. It's no longer about "enjoying your buzz"; at some point, it becomes about finding your fix, getting your "medicine." At that point, you're single-minded and obsessed.

It was right around that time that I decided to try to quit drinking again. My life had changed drastically since the last time I had been sober. I was in an amazing relationship with someone who would go on to become my wife. I had found investors for my fund and was an investor myself. The world was getting to know my work and the Backstage brand. But I still couldn't shake the need to drink daily.

I was afraid that I would need to check myself into a rehab facility soon if I couldn't get my drinking under control. I was finding no joy in drinking, and it was really the only thing in my life that I felt still wielded some type of control over me. For me, as an alpha personality, that was not a good feeling.

During that Pride weekend, I did a search for books about sobriety to try one more tactic before going the full-on rehab route (which would have been expensive and a huge distraction to my livelihood). During the search, I stumbled across an audiobook with great reviews called *This Naked Mind*. I figured it wouldn't hurt to try it out, and since it was written and narrated by a woman, I thought I would have an easier time relating to it. I figured the worst that could happen was that it wouldn't work and I would have wasted a few dollars and hours of my time.

I started the book the day before going to Summer 2017 Pride and finished it five days later. I have not had a drink since then.

SINCE TIME IS MONEY, GOING SOBER HAS BEEN A GREAT INVESTMENT.

Here's some of the stuff I've noticed since I stopped drinking:

1. I've stopped pretending to enjoy small talk. I can talk to myself or to another person for hours if you let me. I have no trouble finding things to talk about. But behind it all, I am an introvert who likes her solitude. When you're out at a bar or club drinking, you tend to engage in some wasteful conversation at times either to be polite or to pass time. I also can't count

the number of times I pretended to be interested in someone's conversation because they'd shelled out $6 for a drink for me. The one thing I never did was romantically flirt or lead anyone on for a drink. But I've definitely engaged in my fair share of platonic giggles and hair tosses with strangers at a bar at four in the afternoon on a Wednesday.

2. I'm able to differentiate between true friends and drinking buddies. I found that once the fog lifted, I became better at sussing out people's intentions in general. That skill had probably always been there, but had been vodka soaked for far too long.

3. I learned that I'm actually a morning person! I wake up hella early now, around 6:00 or 7:00 A.M., instead of groggily pounding the snooze button at 9:00 A.M. for an hour. Since my body doesn't have to metabolize all of the poison throughout the night, I don't wake up every two hours uncomfortable and in most cases swaying as though I'm on an invisible boat. A better night's sleep leads to a more refreshed and easily accessible morning. Since time is money, going sober has been a great investment.

4. Food tastes so much better, and colors are more vibrant. My senses are doing their jobs rather than being flooded with numbing sauce. Did you know that food is delicious? I had no idea.

5. I am more patient. I still don't suffer fools easily, but I am more tolerant of people's idiosyncrasies and definitely treat my friends and family better.

6. I'm more clever and creative. When I tried to stop drinking in the past, I was always afraid that the art-

ist in me would not be the same. I had romanticized the relationship one has with alcohol or even marijuana as it relates to thoughts and imagination, and I thought surely I would never be funny again or never write as well or have as many ideas as I was used to having. But a funny thing happened: my work got even better than before. I'm the most creative and capable I've ever been.

7. My balance is better, and I feel more in control of my body. I'm still no Olympic hopeful, but I feel much more secure with my footing these days. I had no idea how bad my balance was, but I often stumbled or suffered from dizziness even if I hadn't started drinking that day. It was years and years of damage to my nervous system that was causing it, and after a few months of being sober, I started noticing a marked change.

8. I am less paranoid, have fewer regrets, and feel less shame. This speaks for itself.

9. I probably saved my relationship from ending. My wife, Anna, who was my girlfriend at the time, is a remarkable human being. She's what we in the industry call the bee's knees. She's also one of the most tolerant, reasonable, and understanding people I've ever encountered. I often call her "Yoda" and compare her to a Buddhist monk, a German philosopher, or a spiritual guru. But here's the thing: she also has her limits, and my nonsense was not going to work forever. Having to deal with my shortness while drunk or listen to my breathing while I slept to make sure I was still alive, that was some heavy stuff. I wouldn't have wanted her to have to deal with that,

either. It was one of the major reasons I sought help. She might have a beer or a glass of wine every month or five, but we enjoy countless fun sober days and nights together without either of us feeling as though we're missing a thing. We were married on August 14, 2019.

10. No. More. Hangovers. GIRL, did you hear me?

28

Focus on Your Hobby to Sharpen Your Lens

Chase what inspires, invigorates, and refuels you.
If you do that, success will find you.
It will chase you in return.

Caring for yourself has positive effects on all aspects of your life. Though spending eighteen hours a day working on a project can feel as though it will lead to a better product at the end of the day, it can often have the opposite effect. Taking a step away from a project can enable you to see it with fresh eyes.

TAKING A STEP AWAY
FROM A PROJECT CAN
ENABLE YOU TO SEE IT
WITH FRESH EYES.

For me, taking a step away from my work to indulge in a creative hobby really improves my work. It's important to give time to something you're passionate about, something you do for your enjoyment, interest, and creativity alone. It should be something that isn't related directly to your job. It shouldn't be a means to an end. We tend to think that if something isn't making us money, could one day make us money, or gives us opportunities to socialize, it must be less worthwhile. In the start-up world especially, it's easy to confuse a hobby with the search for the next big idea, the idea that you're so passionate about that you want to spend every moment on it. This is not the kind of hobby I am talking about. It's vital that your hobby be something you can do without being concerned about results, revenue, or what other people think. You're doing it just for you. You don't even need to be good at it. That's what's great about a hobby; the only prerequisites are passion and enthusiasm.

> GIVE TIME TO SOMETHING
> YOU'RE PASSIONATE
> ABOUT, SOMETHING THAT
> YOU DO FOR YOUR ENJOYMENT,
> INTEREST, AND CREATIVITY ALONE.

As children, we are encouraged to paint, to draw, to dance, to sing, to be creative in all kinds of ways. But at some point we put those things aside; we become somewhat embarrassed to do them if we aren't "good" at them. As adults we—especially women—tend to avoid doing things we aren't amazing at, even if we used to enjoy them. This is very unfortunate. We all have different passions, interests, and degrees of freedom when it comes to time and money, so this isn't a one size fits all. A hobby doesn't always have to cost you money; I've always had some kind of hobby I do to blow off steam, even when I was broke. And it doesn't have to be something you do every day; it could be a once-a-month kind of endeavor. Regardless of what it is or how much time you devote to it, it's important for your mind to have something to concentrate on other than work.

For me, it's photography. I wasn't a good photographer when I was young. In fact, I was known for my bad photos. I'd be the one who cut people's heads out of the picture, captured them red-eyed, or made everyone look blurry. Yet I see things in photographs; it's how I view the world. So when I had the opportunity to take a photography class for a few months at a local college, I took it. I was twenty at the time and barely had any money, but I managed to get an old camera from a pawnshop. It was a Minolta made in 1980, the same year I was born. No one else in my class had a camera as old or as cheap as mine was, but I loved it. It was heavy, it had all these cool parts to it, and there was no automatic focus; I really had to work at it. The more I learned about photography, the more I enjoyed it. It was like solving a math problem or seeing a puzzle come together piece by piece. I began taking some really great pictures, and they were displayed in our class art shows. That gave me the confidence to start taking more photos of people, even people I didn't know.

Over the years, I have dipped into and out of photography as a hobby, depending on my situation. Recently I've gotten back into it in a big way, and it's been great for my soul and my work. Part of the reason I got back into it is that now I travel all the time; in 2018, I traveled three hundred days. It's great to have a camera on me, even if just my phone's camera, so I can experiment with ways to capture the crazy journey that I'm on. I love how, wherever I am, I can take myself out for however long I need to and just think about photography; the camera becomes the lens through which I see the place I'm in and the people around me. It's grounding, it's refreshing, and it's fun.

WHEN YOUR QUALITY OF LIFE IMPROVES, YOUR WORK IMPROVES.

Having a hobby like that—something that feeds your soul, makes you feel accomplished and invigorated—improves your quality of life. When your quality of life improves, your work improves. Your hobby gives your mind time to think about something else, and when you're concentrating on that other enjoyable thing, your subconscious is working for you. When I'm struggling with a challenge at work, I'll take a couple of hours to pay attention to something else that engages another part of my mind. Once I've done that and I return to my work, things are clearer. Making decisions is easier. Ideas and insights are brought to the foreground.

Everyone needs a hobby that they love as much as I love photography. It'll sharpen your mind, widen your perspective, and help bring more of your life into focus.

29

You Are Your Greatest Investment

am often asked: How should I invest my money? Which companies are going to give me the best return? What's the best bet for me? My answer is simple: You are your best bet.

YOU ARE
YOUR BEST BET.

Obviously, as a venture capitalist, I believe in investing in companies, technology, and people. But I also believe that you should always be your number one investment. A friend recently texted me asking how she should invest $10,000 of her personal capital. This was my reply:

Here's my suggestion . . . you use $5,000 to invest elsewhere, and you use $5,000 to invest in yourself. The ROI (return on investment) on investing in yourself can be immeasurable. So you slice it into categories like: education, experience, self-care.

Education could be books that you buy at Barnes & Noble about business and investing or on Audible that you listen to on your commute. It can also be online workshops and access to platforms like creativelive .com, MasterClass, Udemy, and Lynda.com.

Experience can be an out of town conference that you wouldn't normally spend the money on, but that could be a huge turning point for you. Or it could be several smaller local events that you buy tickets to, either in your field or in the field you want to learn the most about.

Self-care is about recognizing your value. That means valuing yourself enough to take a vacation to help relax you or even spending a night at a hotel in a town where you can clear your mind for a weekend. It's using those vacation days that you normally don't take to start writing your book, graduating from that chapter you've been working on for a couple of years so you can really get on with the process.

Or you could invest in other women and give five women $1,000 seed money to work on their project.

SELF-CARE IS
ABOUT RECOGNIZING
YOUR VALUE.

Make it a priority to invest in these things, and they'll help you decide what else to invest in. That's my holistic view of what I'd do with $10,000.

PART VIII

THE BIG PICTURE

30

Being Part of the Picture

The world is about to watch Black founders go from
"Can you see me?" to "Watch me!"

n October 2018, I made my own piece of history. I became
the first Black woman who is not an entertainer or athlete
to grace the print cover of *Fast Company* magazine. Before
me, there were Oprah, Serena Williams, and Beyoncé. Talk
about good company!

For those who don't know it, *Fast Company* is a magazine
about business and innovation with a circulation of around
700,000 and a massive online presence (to the tune of 36 million average monthly page views and 11 million unique visitors each month). More important, it's a magazine that I read
and respect. I read *Fast Company* when I was broke: when I
first started learning about Silicon Valley, before Backstage
Capital even existed, let alone had any investors. I never could
have imagined myself on the front cover.

When I was interviewed for the magazine, I didn't know if I would be the cover story. I was told the people there were deciding between me and two other people. I was asked to do a photo shoot in New York City, which turned out to be a full-on production, as I was going to have a four-to-six-page spread in the print edition whether I got the cover or not. That was really a big deal at the time. I'm not someone who does many photo shoots; I usually prefer to be the one behind the camera rather than in front of it.

I was going to fly to New York from Los Angeles, my home, connecting in Detroit. When I arrived in Detroit, I was told that the flight to New York had been postponed due to bad weather. That was a problem. The photo shoot was the next morning, and I had to be there. I thought about renting a car, but that would have meant roughly ten hours of driving overnight. And then who knows what I would have looked or felt like when I arrived. I considered flying out in the morning first thing, but I didn't want to risk it in case the flight was still delayed or the weather got worse.

I quickly made the decision to fly to Washington, DC, on the last flight out, and then first thing in the morning I'd get on the Amtrak from DC to New York. I wasn't going to have my luggage because it would still be in Detroit. The airline said it would try to deliver the bag to me in the morning at my New York hotel. So I flew to DC, stayed at a hotel near the airport, got maybe four or five hours of sleep, and then was on my way to the train station.

I took a three-hour train to New York Penn Station, jumped into a car, went to the hotel, checked with the front desk, and learned it had no luggage for me. I called the airline, which confirmed that my bag was *not* on its way. It contained the new clothes I had bought for the potential cover shoot, all of my toiletries, my comb, everything. And I had maybe two hours before I needed to be at the studio. So I did what one does in such a situation: I asked my hairstylist and old makeup artist friend of mine to meet me at the hotel with my friend and co-worker Dianne. Then I ran out to Rite Aid and picked up some toiletries while they went out and bought me some clothes. They styled me on the spot.

The photo shoot took about two hours; the magazine needed three or four photographs to use in the article and perhaps one shot for the cover. There were three costume changes and three backdrop changes, and throughout I listened to music by Nicki Minaj, Rihanna, and Janine on my iPhone. I was out of my element, and it was a strange experience. But the photographer and his team were amazing, and the *Fast Company* team was incredibly supportive and helpful.

My main fear was that I wouldn't have control over what the final photographs looked like. I worried that they might lighten the photograph or alter it heavily to make me seem more "polished." What I love about the cover photo they used is that it looks like me. I'm wearing makeup and I have fewer blemishes, but I recognize myself, which is really important to me. I also love that I'm wearing a standard black shirt and looking directly at the camera; there are no distractions.

When the magazine was published, I was in the middle of a speaking tour that took me to many different states. As a result, I spent a lot of time in airports, where I'd see my face on the magazine shelf in the newsstands. I got a kick out of seeing it every time, but especially when it happened to be shelved next to another magazine with a powerful Black woman on the front. Seeing my face on the cover of *Fast Company* positioned directly below Janet Jackson on the cover of *InStyle* magazine was incredible.

Full disclosure: I also bought a lot of copies of October's *Fast Company*. I bought the magazine wherever and whenever I saw it and gave out copies to people at the events I attended. Some of the most rewarding experiences were the interactions I had with cashiers, most of whom were women of color. I'd arrive at the checkout with a pile of magazines, and they'd ask me questions and congratulate me as if we were family. The support of those women, whom I did not know, was unparalleled. Their reactions were wonderful. Many of them didn't know anything about Silicon Valley or venture capital, but they sure understood what it meant to have a Black woman on the front cover of a business magazine.

Looking at the covers of other business and tech magazines, you would think there weren't any Black women in business at all. As an experiment, I once looked through a year's worth of issues of *Inc., Wired, Entrepreneur, Fortune, Forbes, Money,* and *Fast Company* and found that aside from me, there were only three Black women on the cover of those seven publications combined. One was Venus Williams, and each of the other two was part of a group shot. I went back another year; Venus Williams was featured on the cover of *Inc.* in February 2017. That's it.

During that same tour, I was invited to speak at a *Forbes* Under 30 Summit in Boston (the same one I'd had to turn down two years prior due to stage fright!). I was staying in a nice hotel, and upon arrival I was upgraded to a beautiful suite. When I was leaving my room to head to the event, a woman in the hallway stopped me and asked me a question that made it clear she thought I was a housekeeper; that when she saw me coming out of a suite in a fancy hotel, her first thought was "Oh, this must be the maid." I stood outside my room and asked her to repeat herself, at which point she realized her mistake and was clearly very embarrassed. I don't believe there was any malicious intent behind her question. But it reminded me: you can be the founder of a multimillion-dollar venture firm, speaking at a *Forbes* event, on the cover of a magazine, and still it will take less than a minute for someone to remind you that you're still a Black woman in America.

WHEN YOU EXPAND PEOPLE'S PERCEPTION OF WHAT IS POSSIBLE, YOU ENABLE THEM TO THINK BOLDER, DREAM BIGGER, AND ACHIEVE MORE.

Assumptions like this one are the reason magazine covers are so important. It's why representation in all media is important. Black people have widely varied lives; we are complex, interesting, creative, and smart, yet our representation in the media is still incredibly narrow. Having a Black woman on the cover of *any* magazine is still something newsworthy. The September 2018 Black woman takeover of the fashion industry, in which Beyoncé, Rihanna, Issa Rae, Lupita Nyong'o, Slick Woods, Zendaya, Tracee Ellis Ross, and Tiffany Haddish all appeared on the covers of fashion magazines, caused a lot of excitement on Black Twitter. Imagine if every time there was a White woman on the cover of a magazine, people were talking about it and going out to buy it, whether they usually buy the magazine or not. Black women are searching for role models. They're searching to see themselves in different settings. When you expand people's perception of what is possible, you enable them to think bolder, dream bigger, and achieve more.

In all honesty, I don't want to be the "first" or "one of the only." I want Black women on the cover of business magazines (and magazines in general) to be totally normal. I want to go to the newsstands and see people such as Jewel Burks Solomon, Stephanie Lampkin, Jessica O. Matthews, Sheena Allen, and Morgan DeBaun looking at me from the stacks. I already know these powerful, innovative, awe-inspiring women. They inspire me daily. What I want is for other Black women to find out about all of them and be inspired, too. I want to end the myth that the only way to be successful in business is to be a straight White man. Thanks to magazines like *Fast Company, Essence,* and *The Atlantic,* this is happening more often than I've ever seen in the past.

I DON'T WANT TO BE THE EXCEPTION TO THE RULE; I WANT THE RULES TO ACCEPT ME.

What I'm doing with Backstage Capital is amplifying the talent that already exists and ensuring that people know about it. I'm asking that business and tech magazines do the same. I don't want to be the exception to the rule; I want the rules to accept me.

When I first held a physical copy of that issue of *Fast Company* in my hands, I was very emotional. I had a sort of out-of-body experience, just looking at that object and seeing my own face looking back. I had so many thoughts in that moment, but the most powerful one was "What would I have done if I had seen a face like mine on the cover of this magazine a few years ago?" Back when I was learning about venture capital, I was looking for a mentor, looking for an employer, but more than anything else, I was looking for representation. I was looking for the people who look like me. When I realized that those people weren't able to get into the rooms they needed to in order to participate in venture capital, I realized I had to create those opportunities. When I see my face on that cover, it's not just my face, it's not just my story—it's all of our stories to come. It's the springboard that reminds a Black woman that she belongs in whatever room she wants to be in: she's business savvy, she's smart, and she's going to take a chance.

It's about Black women who decide to start a company because they know, because they've seen, that Black women do that. And it's about the future, when a Black woman coming out of a nice hotel room isn't synonymous with "housekeeper."

There is nothing wrong with being a housekeeper. That is not the point. If I had been White, would she have made the assumption?

31

The Glory Days

There's a lot of power in understanding why you're doing something.

No one ever said that running a company isn't stressful. In fact, no one ever said *life* isn't stressful, especially when you're underestimated in all that you do. When I started Backstage Capital, I never could have guessed we'd have Donald Trump in the White House. With all the racism and hate in the news all the time, it can often feel like a full-time job just keeping up with it all. And it's us, the people of color, women, the LGBTQ+ community, who are hit the hardest by new policies, by the dangerous rhetoric, by the encouragement of the radical right wing. So how can we keep looking forward, when it seems in many ways as though we're moving backward? How can we stay positive and keep going on the worst of days? How can those of us who feel constantly worn down by the news continue to smile, to strive, to plan, and to do?

The first step is to decide *why* you're doing what you're doing—whether it's teaching, raising your children, working creatively, working in food service, or founding a company. Ask yourself, "Why do I care about this? What is my mission? What does the big picture look like?" Knowing what your intentions are will help you bring about your goals; you can't reach your goals if you don't know what they are. Reminding yourself why you do what you do is imperative. It enables you to look past the microaggressions and concentrate on your journey.

A few days after President Trump was elected, after I had spent some time reeling from it and trying to take care of myself while working out what it all meant and what this new world was, I decided that now, more than ever, I would have to aim for unbridled success. I decided that my success would *be* my activism. It would be success that could catalyze the success of others. In truth, what I want, what I'm aiming for with Backstage Capital, is to be so successful that we're no longer needed. I want to put myself out of business by eradicating the need for a company that invests in the underestimated. In my big picture, when I look to the future, we're no longer underestimated.

HYPE, RECOGNITION,
AND MONEY CAN
ALL BE FLEETING;
I'M DRIVEN BY IMPACT,
LEGACY, AND DIGNITY.

I don't want to be a lone, rich, Black, gay woman. I want to see so many people who look like me succeeding. Hype, recognition, and money can all be fleeting; I'm driven by impact, legacy, and dignity.

EACH UNDERESTIMATED FOUNDER DOES NOT HAVE TO BE *THE ONLY* ROLE MODEL, THE *ONLY CHANCE* EACH GROUP OF PEOPLE GETS.

But as much as I want underestimated founders to succeed, I also want there to be space for them to fail. I want these founders to have the same learning curve, the second and third chances that White male investors get. Each underestimated founder does not have to be *the only* role model, the *only chance* each group of people gets.

I'm not in this just to become incredibly wealthy. I'm in this for the glory days. I'm here for the day when I look over and see a Backstage portfolio company prepping for its IPO and know that part of the reason it's on that path is because of our efforts. I'm in this to watch more DIY hair care companies like Curl Mix go from less than $10,000 in revenue per month to more than $1 million per month two years after taking on our $25,000 investment. These are the kinds of stories that will make the tough times I've gone through and the tough days ahead worth it.

We can see it. We can see it on the horizon. We can see when we meet a Black woman from Atlanta who says, "I started a company that has generated revenue because I read about Backstage a year prior." We see it when we meet customers of a portfolio company and they're very excited about and happy with their product. We see it when we meet a Latina angel investor who says, "I didn't realize I was allowed to make angel investments in start-up companies. Now I have a piece of equity and I can impart my wisdom and my skill to someone else." We see it anytime we meet someone who says, "I didn't know I was invited to the table, and now I've earned my place there." We go through all of the ups and downs, all of the degradation, just for that.

That *Fast Company* cover article described me as part of the "new guard." Soon after, someone on Twitter wrote that instead of thinking of me as a new type of gatekeeper, people should think of me as a key maker. I loved that and couldn't agree more. Being a key maker is all about understanding your privilege and sharing it to lift others up. Privilege isn't a bad word. There is nothing wrong with having privilege. Some people have inherent privilege that comes from race, gender, background, or wealth, but privilege is also something you can gain in many different ways. I now have the privilege of being known as the founder of Backstage Capital. People are more likely to listen to me because I have gained a certain status in the community. I understand that, and I try to use that privilege to help others step up to the platform I've been given. If you're trying to understand how to share your inherent privilege, think back to the lesson from chapter 8: when someone shorter than you needs to see the stage better at a show, you usually let them stand in front of you, right? You both get to enjoy the show, it's only a slight inconvenience for you, and, most important, you don't shrink because of it.

There is a big difference between privilege and entitlement. I think of it this way: privilege is a hand-me-down heirloom, rooted in the circumstances you were born into.

Entitlement is something you procure and choose to wear. The meaning of life to me is doing as much for other people as possible for as long as possible. Give, replenish, give more. I don't envy other underrepresented investors who succeed, I celebrate them! I'm propelled by the movement, not just by personal or brand success.

I want to create generational wealth. I want to secure the health and welfare of not only the founders we're investing in but their children and grandchildren, too. I want to help create a new guard of powerful women, powerful people of color, powerful LGBTQ+ people. By creating wealth for groups that historically have not had that kind of economic stability, we will change the economic dynamics and therefore the power dynamics of our industry. We will have changed not only our industry but also the power dynamics in the United States and in the world at large. That's how far-reaching this could be. That's what I'm aiming for. That's what the glory days mean to me.

What do your glory days look like? Can you sketch them out? Can you see the future clearly? Can you draw the map that will get you there? Once you can do this, you're on your way.

32

Don't Call It a Comeback

One early morning in March 2019, I woke up in a cold sweat, gravely concerned. There had recently been yet another investor who left negotiations in the millions of dollars after months of diligence, and I wasn't sure where we were going to find the capital we needed at the time.

Then suddenly, a great calm washed over me as I had yet another silent "talk-me-down" conversation with myself. I sat on a chair on my balcony overlooking east Hollywood and Downtown LA, wearing a robe and letting the sunlight hit my bare legs. I realized in that moment that I hadn't sat still for this long or let the sunlight bathe me anywhere in months. I was for the first time in a long time, calm, content, and at peace. I knew the solution. I'd had an epiphany.

I walked back into my apartment and called my business partner and Backstage general partner Christie Pitts, who was at her home in Oakland. I said, "I need to do less. I need less work, and fewer worries, if I'm going to be able to continue to perform at the quality and pace and impact I do now. I think the way I can open up more time and freedom for me to do this is for you to become CEO of Backstage Studio, while I remain co-founder of Studio and founder and managing partner of Backstage Capital."

Christie thought for only a moment and said, "I'd be honored! Yes, I can do that." This was a big moment for both of us because we both knew that it was the right decision. It was during a time where we were figuring out our long-term sustainability when it came to operating expenses, and what sort of talents and skills we had as a team. Christie and I had cofounded Studio in January 2018 as an angel-backed c-corp arm of Backstage that generates revenue by partnering with corporations, throwing events, and owning the IP in Backstage Accelerator.

The idea for Studio came from me initially, and I tapped Christie to co-found it with me. From day one, we split responsibilities and stakes, and co-led Backstage Studio with everything from seven to forty-five employees and freelancers. In addition to her role with me at Backstage Capital investing in and nurturing companies in our portfolio, Christie had built out Studio's HR platform, made hires, sourced partnerships, and led the internal day-to-day operations. So this request was a natural transition for both of us.

This practice of self-reflection, followed by self-care and execution, was nothing new for me and for us as a company. We adapt and ebb and flow as needed, and although we don't always get it pitch perfect, we do strive to practice an open, inclusive, thoughtful, and reflective leadership style.

I let the rest of the team know of the technical change via a video conference call and prepared our stakeholder messaging. I recorded an audio clip for our investors where I outlined where my focus would be best suited—or as Justin Kan and others say, where my "zone of genius" was: 1) escalated fundraising, 2) supporting our current portfolio of more than one hundred companies by connecting them with follow-on funders, new customers, and helping with recruiting, and 3) building on Backstage's branding and reach through more speaking, podcasting, writing, and other media. The audio clip was prepped to go out later in the week.

To me, this was a stroke of genius. Christie would be given more credit for her work, and I would be given fewer day-to-day and administrative duties. Simply put: I would go from doing the work of six people to the work of three. And I would be doing what I do best, what I'm best aligned with, and what I love most, which would in turn create the most positive impact to Backstage, our founders, and our investors: I would be practicing self-care.

A couple of days after having this epiphany, and setting the new structure into motion, we at Backstage woke up to this headline and newsletter subject line from Dan Primack at *Axios:* "Arlan Hamilton's Diversity-Minded Fund Falls Through."

Falls through? I started looking around in faux confusion like in the Whitney Houston gif. The fund fell through? When? It turns out that Dan's take was that because we hadn't yet raised the $36 million fund to invest $1 million at a time into Black-women-led companies—which we'd announced we were raising in May 2018—it had somehow become a failure on this particular day.

The article made no mention of the one hundred plus companies we had invested in in less than three years, the millions of dollars I'd single-handedly raised, or the fact that more than half of venture funds take more than one year to hit their target. Another angle Dan seemed to revel in was the idea that I was and had always been "overhyped." A media darling with a rags to riches story that had always rung slightly too good to be true to him. Someone online referred to his style of reporting in this particular article as "gleeful," which I have to agree with.

I immediately started getting condolences texts and emails from strangers and friends alike. In order to set the record straight to stakeholders, I drafted an email letting everyone know I was okay, Backstage was okay, and that there was no news in this news piece. In the email, I attached the audio clip I had prepared two days earlier, to let them know all of the good news we had. Their fearless leader wouldn't be as stressed anymore! Yay! Yay? Anyone?

Well, that email and audio clip were, for some reason, leaked to *Fortune,* by one of our investors (or teammates?), who was claiming that I had left Backstage! Um . . . lol, when? So the unflattering headlines exploded. The fire was ignited, the inaccurate narrative was ablaze, and there was no containing it now.

The irony is that the stress that these internal changes were designed to relieve was now compounded by this mess, and life had just gotten *more* difficult, unnecessarily. My mental, emotional, spiritual, and physical health were already suffering, and now this was like gasoline thrown on top.

A few things helped me during that time. One was a hashtag trending in the San Francisco area the same day: #LetArlanKnow, which hundreds and hundreds of people used to let me know how I had positively impacted their lives. It was started with people who had found the reporting to be biased and unfair, and wanted me to know that they weren't buying into it or giving it much weight. That meant so much to me. For the people writing the headlines and the articles, it was just one of a dozen they'd write that month. But for me, it was a catalyst for a bombardment of bad energy, thrown my way from people who didn't have all the facts. I had already been teetering on the edge of needing a break while dealing with an unhealthy amount of stress. So hearing from all of these lovely people helped me understand quickly that I need not worry about the aesthetics.

I still get people asking me how my "vacation" from Backstage is going, or saying how nice it must be to be "retired" now. And I just stare blankly at them like, *Girlfriend, tell that to my sixteen-hour days and my four-flights-in-a-week schedule.* But these days I laugh it off and explain that it was inaccurate reporting. I understand where some of it was coming from, and I don't think any of the journalists are bad people. I am a huge proponent of the first amendment and of people having their voice heard—even when it is dissenting of mine.

I got to speak my peace on PBS's *Amanpour & Company* with Alicia Menendez a few days later, which was really helpful, and then again in more detail on Bloomberg's *Studio 1.0* with Emily Chang. (I, by the way, was the first Black woman featured on that show, and won't be the last if I have anything to do with it).

This is part of the transcript from my PBS interview:

MENENDEZ: There is news that I want you to respond to this week. "Axios's" Dan Primack broke news that the $36 million, "It's About Damn Time" fund, has fallen through. That was a fund intended to invest solely in Black female founders; "fallen through," his words, not mine. "The bottom line, Hamilton," you, "has a compelling biography and she has sought to do something laudable outside of Silicon Valley's pattern matching mold. But it is also true that tech media has been so thirsty for such stories that it may have put the cart before the horse, attributing success to a work very much still in progress." How do you respond?

HAMILTON: Yes. Well, first of all, the "fallen through" part of the headline was very shocking to me. I talked to so many [people who are raising funds] who are going through the exact same thing I'm going through. I can understand if you're outside of Silicon Valley, you're outside of venture, if you're not as educated as Dan is, thinking on the subject, thinking oh, well, they said they had a fund, they don't have a fund right now so they must have failed. But he is too smart for that. And I don't really understand it. So I don't accept the failed part of it. It's almost like saying your flight from L.A. to New York has not landed yet, therefore, it's a failure. It hasn't landed yet. That's all it is.

MENENDEZ: It's not the only news this week. We've also learned you're stepping down as CEO of Backstage Studio.

HAMILTON: Studio, yes.

MENENDEZ: Which is the firm's venture studio that incubates new companies and products.

HAMILTON: Yes. And it runs our operations.

MENENDEZ: And that Christie Pitts, your partner and chief of staff, will now be in charge of Backstage Studio.

HAMILTON: Absolutely.

MENENDEZ: So what does that shake up?

HAMILTON: OK. So I'm glad you asked. So Backstage Studio is something that we launched. Christie and I cofounded it a little over a year ago to keep the lights on and keep going so that we could continue to support our portfolio of a hundred plus companies. I'll say that again. Most funds do not have that many companies [in their portfolio]. So the stepping down as CEO part, I went into it as CEO. Christie was my co-founder. We worked together every day on many things and she's just a remarkable person. I have taken on the role of too many people at Backstage. I take on too much. I talk about self-care almost every day online. I tell people, take care of yourself. If you don't take care of yourself, how can you take care of others?

MENENDEZ: And you're not taking care of yourself?

HAMILTON: I had been trying, but then I reached a point where I'm like, I am too stressed day to day about the tiniest things. It only makes sense.

MENENDEZ: And also—I think for those of us watching, it also raises the question, can you be the brand and do the work?

HAMILTON: Right. So, this is—to me, honestly, this is just an evolution. I love launching things. I love catalyzing. I love inspiring. I love working with our founders to help them get more resources that they deserve. I love all of that. I love sitting one on one with founders and just working through a problem with them. I have a difficult time being able to do that as much as I want when I'm over here worrying about the price of office supplies. It's just really basic. And it's not a big story. To me, it's practicing what I preach. I feel like I haven't even begun and there is so much more for me to do.

MENENDEZ: Arlan, thank you so much.

HAMILTON: Thank you. Appreciate it.

33

A Letter to the Reader

recently took a two-day vacation to Laguna Beach with my wife, Anna. From our hotel room, we had an absolutely gorgeous, expansive view of the beach and the water. The horizon seemed to be a million miles away and at our feet at the same time. On our last morning there after watching the sunrise by myself on the balcony, I listened to music on my headphones and watched the tides rip and roll. For several minutes, I observed the peaceful water patterns and wondered how long it would take something to happen deep into the horizon for the effect to be seen at shore. If a boat shifted course miles out into the water, how long would it take one of its waves to reach the sand?

I then started to reflect on something Anna had said to me earlier on the trip: that the sea has been there for thousands of years before us and will be there when we're gone. (My wife and I are the most stoned-conversation-having people who no longer smoke weed you've ever seen!)

Similarly, something my mom said to me while we were on

one of our road trips—this time post-fund and with plenty of gas money—came to mind: "The seed doesn't see the petal." She'd heard this somewhere and believed it was an ancient Chinese proverb but wasn't entirely sure.

So two things I know: 1) the journey we're on today, with its twists and turns, will take some time to reach the shore, and 2) we may not get to see the full breadth—the petal or the wave—of all of our work, as we are part of the seeds and the horizon.

Those two things help ground me and set me to flight at the same time. They help me understand that this is bigger than me, and it's bigger than you, because it's about *us*. So when I have a bad call, or hear an unkind word, or even have a bad year, if I remind myself of these simple truths, I am once again reminded of my resolve, fortified in my conviction, and can press on.

These concepts also help me dream bigger and brighter than ever before. There is no limit to what I believe today's underestimated can achieve over the next few decades. Imagining a Black woman reading this years in the future, as an artifact of the way things once were in business, gives me enough fuel to last my lifetime. And to think those years and decades can start with you today as you close this book.

So press on, I beg of you, we are in this together. When I win, you win. When you win, I win. And when we win, we ALL win.

34

Frequently Asked Questions

am regularly contacted by people who are looking for information about start-ups, venture capital, and investing. When I was learning about this industry, books were my starting point, so I'd like *this* book to be the same kind of helpful tool for its readers. Here are the questions I am asked most often and the answers I give. Use this as a starting point, and then check out the other books mentioned here if you'd like to know more.

What are investors looking for in a company?

AN INVESTMENT SHOULD
FEEL AS THOUGH IT'S GOING
TO RETURN AT LEAST TEN TIMES
THE AMOUNT OF MONEY
THAT AN INVESTOR PUTS IN.

Different investors are going to have different criteria and tastes. When you are talking to investors, you have to keep in mind the timing of their fund, the timing of their own raise, the availability of their capital, and many other factors. Most investors in the venture capital and angel investor spaces are looking for companies that they believe can return a significant amount of capital to them if their plans are well executed. One law is that an investment should feel as though it's going to return at least ten times the amount of money that an investor puts in. It's up to you to do your research, to learn everything you can about the investors you're talking to both individually and at funds. Even within a fund, different partners will have different personalities, criteria, and methods in the way they go about investing.

What do you look for in a founder?

HUNGRY,
NOT THIRSTY.

I'm looking for someone whom I call "hungry, not thirsty," meaning someone who is willing to do what it takes to execute on their vision but is not willing to cross ethical lines or become a bulldozer in response to a desperate situation. It is very important that you be discerning in what you do, how you act, and how you treat others. I look for someone who is kind, respectful, and diligent, who makes good on their word, and who has integrity and passion for what they are doing. I'm also looking for founders and business owners who remind me of myself; someone whom White male investors may have overlooked. I always say that I pattern match for grit, so I'm looking for someone who is resilient and creative and has integrity. I look for someone who is resourceful and has done a lot with a little.

I PATTERN MATCH
FOR GRIT.

How do you know if you should seek investment?

Generally, you should research and look for capital *before* you need it so that you can put yourself into a position where you aren't desperately searching for capital to keep yourself afloat or keep your business going. This helps ensure that you are in a leveraged position. Runway is the amount of capital and resources that you have to cover your expenses, and is usually measured in months. You should calculate your runway and make sure you have several months in front of you, in the same way a pilot of an airplane knows how much tarmac is left under its wheels when it takes off or lands.

You're going to want to think about seeking investment if you feel okay about the equity—that is, the percentage ownership of a company an investor is going to take from you in exchange for the capital invested. If you think that it's worth their having ownership in your company and in some cases a say in your decisions because their investment will help you scale (aka grow), you're ready to think about taking on outside capital.

You might also seek outside capital if you think that you are in a highly competitive space in which your competitors are well funded and you know you need capital to lure talent— which is probably the most important thing you can spend money on—as well as for marketing and overhead and other things you need to stay in the game. In tech-heavy companies, a lot of money often goes toward the infrastructure needed to run the product or service, whether that means cloud services or the tools needed to build and maintain the underlying technology. Generally, the more users you have, the more it will cost you to run a company.

Keep in mind that a lot of times, especially early on, the necessary digital tools can be bartered for rather than purchased outright. A lot of business-to-business (B2B) companies that sell tools or services to other start-ups are looking to win you over as a customer now, early in your company's life, when you don't have much money, so that you'll be a loyal customer once your company grows. So they will often give you things: free or discounted products for simply having a company and being in business. Seek out those things first.

Do as much as you can through bootstrapping (spending the money that you earn or your own money, within reason, to keep the company going) before you seek or accept outside capital. Generally, you should seek outside capital when you want to grow faster, bigger, and better within a certain amount of time.

What types of investments are available?

I work in the venture capital space. There are also other types of investments, depending on what kind of company you have, what you are already able to do on your own, and what kind of revenue you have. Bootstrapping is a major way a lot of successful people fund their companies based on the income of the company. For instance, let's say you're selling a hair care product or clothing or an app, and the profit that you make you invest right back into the company. You do that for several years, and then you're sailing.

An example of this is Mailchimp, an email and newsletter service a lot of us have heard of. It has more than $600 million in revenue each year, and it has not taken a dime of outside funding. It took the company seventeen years to get to that point, and the first ten years were really lean and tough, but today it doesn't have to share its profits with any investor. It doesn't have to go public if the company owners don't want to. It has autonomy because of its founders' decision not to seek outside funding.

NO MONEY IS FREE UNLESS IT'S BEING HANDED TO YOU AS A GIFT.

Angel investments are another type of capital source. You may have friends and family or people in your network who make a good deal of money or have a good deal of money from their family and who are willing to put a few thousand dollars into your company because they believe in you, they believe in what you're working on, and they want to make a profit. Every time you take money, remember that no money is free unless it's being handed to you as a gift. You are expected to make back that money and more for your investors.

Another way that's really exciting to me is the crowd equity funding space. You've no doubt heard of platforms such as Kickstarter, where you raise $10,000 for your film project, for instance (or if you're supercool, you use the Backstage portfolio company Seed&Spark to do so), and in exchange for someone giving you $50, they will get a T-shirt and a thank-you on the website. That's a really interesting method that has done well over the past several years. With crowd equity funding, a similar thing is happening in that you're looking to a crowd (a mixture of people in your network and strangers), only in this scenario, in exchange for the same $50, someone gets a small piece of ownership in your company.

With the latest regulations that were heralded in the Obama administration and after, that route is becoming more accessible to more people. There was a time when you could invest in companies only if you were accredited, meaning you had to have a certain amount of income per year or a certain amount of money in assets. Now, with new legislation such as the Jobs Act, that has opened up quite a bit. If you're interested in this approach, you will want to dedicate several hours to researching and understanding the process and options, which platforms you can use, and via which regulations you can raise money.

I think that over the next ten years, this and more legislation and policies put into place could explode the angel investment industry and really change the landscape of who funds innovation at its earliest stages. I find the prospect thrilling.

When should you quit your day job to pursue your start-up?

I think a lot of people think that they owe it to someone to go all in, and if they're not 100 percent in on something, it somehow means they're not serious or legitimate. Maybe hustle culture is to blame. Maybe it's just what you're seeing next to you or what you hope for yourself. But I believe that if you have a well-paying job that has health insurance and other benefits and has stability and structure, there's nothing wrong and no shame in holding on to that job while you put the pieces together for your other big thing. I think you can do both at the same time, using the day job to fuel and fund the side hustle in a strategic, responsible, thoughtful way.

It's all about leverage and strategy, right? So you want to put yourself into a position where you can work on things freely without having the added stress of being unable to pay the rent and make ends meet. This setup will enable you to make mistakes, to lose a little bit of money in the name of experimentation and learning. That may mean that you work on your new project a couple of hours after work or before work or you work on it during the weekends, and so on. I think there's no shame in that, and in fact I think it's a really interesting way of testing what you're doing. And then when you get to a point where you're saying, wow, this is actually working, people are liking this, people are spending money on this or they're coming to it in droves, you can start showing that traction to interested parties who will want to help you scale.

Do I need a co-founder? If so, how can I find one?

You don't *need* a co-founder, but I think having a co-founder has a lot of advantages. The start-up journey can be a lonely, stressful, and annoying one. Even if you're doing well, you're still going to have stresses as the stakes get higher, and being able to share and distribute that stress can be extremely valuable—both for you and for your company.

There's also a lot that can be said for going it alone, at least at the beginning, because then you don't have to get permission from someone else to do something you want to or worry about someone else's feelings or concerns. You can be a little bit looser, a little more experimental. It's a lot like traveling; some people have no problem traveling by themselves and in fact prefer that to traveling with someone else because they don't have to travel the way the other person wants to. But it is a little bit more of a lonely experience, and you have to ultimately make key decisions on your own.

If you do decide to get a co-founder and you want to know where to find one, there are a few options. One is to just look in your current network of close friends and sometimes even close family and find someone you have known well for years and worked with on other types of projects. If the two of you executed those projects with very little friction, you may be onto something.

A word of caution: the worst thing you can do is get involved in business with a family member or good friend and have a big blowup that results in your losing your personal connection due to something that was a business transaction. So you want to think about someone you've already tested the waters with in some way. Maybe you have put on an event together that took a few months to plan and went well, or maybe you worked on a project together and it was undeniable that the two of you or the three of you have skills that are really complementary to one another. That could be a good sign that you may work well together again.

Of course, you want to know that the co-founder is as interested and as invested mentally, spiritually, and practically in the company as you are. Therefore you want to find someone who's on the same page as you.

If you don't have such a person in your immediate circle or you don't want to go that route because you're afraid of blowing up an existing relationship, you can find co-founders in other ways. There are websites that help you link up with co-founders, so you could do a search for that. You can go to in-person meetups, conferences, and hackathons, different tech-related events that happen in almost every city these days. Post on social that you're on the lookout for someone. Ask your offline network for referrals.

You don't want to jump in with anyone too quickly, because it is hopefully going to be a long relationship that will result in years and years of your running a company together. If you're just meeting for the first time, you definitely want to have a trial period of several months. You do not have to rush in. You do not have to do anything you don't want to. It's okay to change your mind. It's okay to seek counsel. It's okay to use an intermediary. As discussed in the Self-Care section, your mental, spiritual, and practical well-being are paramount. Proceed accordingly.

How do venture capital firms work?

Venture capital is an asset class within private equity. It's sort of the younger, more defiant sibling who takes big risks, and sometimes those pay off more handsomely than the older, more conservative siblings' lower-risk dealings. The words *firm* and *fund* can be used interchangeably, although most venture capital *firms* manage or are the front office of one or more legal entities (usually LLCs) of pooled funds that are referred to as *funds*.

Let's use a $100 million venture fund that is managed by a venture firm as an example. There are usually three or four general partners at a fund that size, and they manage money that they have spent anywhere from two months to two years raising from outside investors called limited partners. So the venture capitalists you're going around and trying to raise money from had to go around and raise money themselves, which gives a really interesting dynamic to things. Venture capitalists know what it's like to ask for money, and they know what it's like to pitch.

Venture firms tend to raise capital from a few main buckets: high-net-worth individuals (HNIs), family offices, funds of funds, pensions (firefighter or teacher, for instance), foundations and university endowments, insurance companies, and large corporations. The size of the fund will determine which combination of these will be sources for a given fund.

Limited partners do not tend to have a direct say in what companies are being invested in, since they sign up for a general thesis and direction that the general partners have outlined. There is some governance if a majority of the LPs feel that the GPs are mishandling their money or paying themselves exorbitant management fees, and so on.

Once a venture capital fund has been raised, fund managers (the GPs) are tasked with returning that capital to their investors (the LPs) over a period of a decade or so. They do so by making well-informed bets on potential outliers in the hope that one or more of the companies they invest in will return profits so high that they will return an entire fund or more. In a $100 million fund, a significant percentage will usually be used to make follow-up investments into the portfolio companies that do the best over the years. This is a strategy to help funds maintain as much of their original ownership in a company for as long as possible, even through subsequent rounds of funding that dilute the initial investment. In other words, if a GP puts in $1 million in exchange for 10 percent of a company in 2020 and the company sells to Amazon for $100 million in 2030, the investor will want to have at least

$10 million returned. But since the company would most likely have had two or three additional rounds of funding in the meantime, raising the value of the company and therefore lowering (aka diluting) the percentage value of the original $1 million investment each time, the investment firm would need to keep adding to its investment to retain its value. This is accomplished through bargaining rights called "pro rata." You can learn a ton more about this in Brad Feld's book *Venture Deals: Be Smarter Than Your Lawyer and Venture Capitalist*.

So the math works if a company does well, which often leads to an "exit" or some other liquidity event (i.e., the company is bought by some bigger player, usually for a lot of money). When that happens, a fund adds up the total amount it has made over the years and returns 100 percent of the invested money to its investors. In our $100 million fund example, let's say that over ten years a total of six companies out of the thirty the fund invests in go on to have liquidity events that total for the fund, $300 million worth of exits for them.

The first $100 million of that is given back to the limited partners to recoup their original investment. That leaves $200 million in profit (aka "carried interest," aka "carry"). Of that $200 million, the firm takes approximately 20 percent as its commission on the carry. Think of it as being like a tip you might give a dealer at a casino for a great hand, only in this case, the amount is agreed upon well in advance. The GPs take that $40 million and split it among themselves. The $160 million that's left goes to the LP investors so that they are now at 2.6 times net return on their funds.

At the same time, for at least the first half of the ten-year life of the fund, the firm was also charging a management fee. Usually a management fee is 1 to 3 percent of the total amount under management. For our $100 million fund example, an average management fee would be $2 million per year to cover everybody's salary, office rent, travel, SaaS (software as a service), tools, marketing in some cases, and any other overhead needs. The managers are hopefully spending the management fee wisely and responsibly, as it's just a fee for them to be in business.

There is much more to learn about funds, including stacked fees, performance metrics such as TVPI and DPI, succession plans, ecosystem comparisons, and more. Several books, including Brad Feld's *Venture Deals* and Scott Kupor's *Secrets of Sand Hill Road: Venture Capital and How to Get It,* are available for those who want to do a deep dive.

How can I learn more about starting a company or investing in other companies?

Start with my firm's resources page at backstagecapital.com/greenroom. We have spent the past several years putting together all sorts of text, audio, and video resources that address these very questions. We also share interviews, links, a newsletter called *The Mixtape,* and more free resources. I would highly recommend starting there, and then remember that Google is your friend. When you learn a term or hear about a person or get intrigued by some sort of theme, search for it and keep digging. Read archives and the most up-to-date trends and trades. Read ThePLUG by Sherrell Dorsey, a website chock-full of deep data analysis of the venture and investing landscape with a focus on underrepresented communities; the magazines *Fast Company* and *Inc.;* and the websites TechCrunch, Crunchbase, and PitchBook. Reach out to other companies and investors, people who are just a few steps ahead of you. Go to conferences, listen to podcasts (mine is called *Your First Million*!), have monthly meetups with people you meet at those places.

Aspiring investors who have capital, backstagecrowd.com is another resource.

Bottom line, as we've learned in this book: If you want to attract money, you have to *be* money!

INDEX